Social Network Analysis:
An Introduction with an Extensive Implementation to a Large-Scale Online Network Using Pajek

Authored By

Seifedine Kadry

School of Engineering
American University of the Middle East
Kuwait

Co-Author

Mohammed Z. Al-Taie

Computer Science Department
Al-Salam University College in Baghdad
Iraq

DEDICATION

To the soul of my beloved father

Mohammed

To my wife and my angel Hadi

Seifedine

CONTENTS

FOREWORD

SOCIAL NETWORK CULTURE

Social networks, also referred to as social media, include many internet-based tools that help people to comprehend, interact, engage and collaborate with each other. Several social networking platforms such as Facebook, YouTube, LinkedIn, Twitter, and many Web based communities *e.g.* Book Crossing, are being heavily used nowadays in professional life and in some decision making processes.

By its nature, social networking is interactive. You can express your feedback and share your experiences with anyone that you select and *vice versa*. Many businesses recognize the importance of the quality of the provided end-services, but when it comes to embracing the principles of openness and interaction that social networking enables, they may hesitate. After all, there may be just as much unfavorable feedback as there is favorable feedback out there. However, it's the combination of both the positive and the negative that can truly empower organizations to make meaningful changes to enhance the quality of services. Social networks certainly make listening easier, but it's the collection of data and the actions that organizations take that build enduring relationships with customers [Karen Quintos].

WHY SOCIAL NETWORK ANALYSIS?

Social networks operate on several levels, from individuals, families, and groups up to the level of nations, and play a critical role in determining the way problems are handled, organizations are run, and the degree to which individuals achieve their goals. Social network theory maps these relationships between individual actors. Though relatively new on the scene it has become very influential across the social sciences and became a powerful methodological tool alongside statistics.

Assuming no prior knowledge of quantitative sociology, this book presents the key ideas in context through examples and case studies. Using a structured approach to understanding work in this area, Drs. Al-Taie and Kadry suggest further reading and online sources so readers can develop their knowledge and skills to become practitioners of this research area. The authors show how we can practically analyze an on-line community, from different sides, using techniques of social network analysis and learn how to extract the main features of that network.

This reference provides a broad overview on the problem of Social Network Analysis with an extensive implementation to a large-scale online network using Pajek. The analysis deals with a well-known Web-based community that is *'Book Crossing'*.

The book is intended for students and non-specialist readers who want to learn the basics and the applications of social network analysis and not its mathematical properties. The book can also be an enriching source for researchers and practitioners aiming at understanding how the process of large-scale network analysis goes on by providing them with a set of useful techniques that have been developed in the last few years.

Aziz M. Barbar
Dean, Faculty of Arts & Sciences
American University of Science and Technology
Beirut, Lebanon

PREFACE

Social network analysis focuses on ties among people, groups of people, organizations and countries. These ties combine to form networks. It has become a powerful methodological tool alongside statistics.

The book lies in a series of textbooks that explain the principles of social network analysis. Furthermore, it gives the reader a complete application knowledge to perform a large-scale network analysis. Interested readers can apply the analysis techniques used in this book to other online social communities, such as Facebook, MySpace, *etc.*

The book consists of two main parts. The first part (part I) gives the elementary concepts of social network analysis, while the second part (part II) represents the methodological and the practical portion of the book.

The first part starts with an introduction to the main concepts used in this field, such as types of networks, graph theory, social networks and social network analysis, properties of networks *etc.* Then, it is followed by a brief description to some of the common tools that are used by scientists and researchers to analyze networks. Among those are Pajek, UCINET, Network Workbench and others.

Then, it moves to show where social network analysis can be applied, as it can be useful in a number of fields such as recommender systems, business, software development, health, animal social networks and so on.

The second part of the book is dedicated to show how we can practically analyze an on-line community, from different sides, using techniques of social network analysis and learn how to deduce the main features of that network, with the help of Pajek, a tool used to analyze and visualize large-scale networks. The analysis deals with a well-known Web-based community that is *'Book Crossing'*.

Book Crossing website is a place where people, of different ages and from different locations (who are interested in reading books), put their ratings for the books they read. Thus, users supply important information and provide the opportunity for others to make use of the feedback with no need to buy the book beforehand.

The processing of that website comes from two angles: The first angle focuses on the direct relations between users and books. Many things can be inferred from this part of the analysis such as who is more interested in book reading and why? Which books are most popular and which users are most active and why?

What does it mean when two users like the same book? Is it the same as when two other users like thousand books instead of just one? Who is more likely to be a friend with whom and why? Is there any person in the community who is more qualified to establish large circles of social relations? These questions (and others) are to be answered throughout the other part of the analysis, which will take us to probe the potential social relations that exist within this community. Although these relationships are not showing explicitly, they can be induced with the help of affiliation network analysis and techniques such as m-slice and ego-network analyses.

The book is intended for students and public readers who want to learn the basics of social network analysis without going deep into its mathematical and statistical methods. We believe that many of them are interested in the application of social network analysis rather than in its mathematical properties. Therefore, part I of the book can be a good reference for them. The book is also good for researchers and practitioners aiming at understanding how the process of large-scale network analysis goes on. The second part of the book is probably more interesting to them.

For readers who want to extend their knowledge in this field, we refer to other books such as *Social Network Analysis: Methods and Applications,* by Stanley Wasserman and Katherine Faust, *Models and Methods in Social Network Analysis* by Carrington, Scott and Wasserman, *Exploratory Social Network Analysis with Pajek* by Wouter de Nooy, Andrej Mrvar and Vladimir Batagelj. Finally, a concise history of social network analysis can be found in *The Development of Social Network Analysis: A study in the Sociology of Science* by Linton C. Freeman.

ACKNOWLEDGEMENTS

We would like to thank all reviewers for their insightful and valuable comments that improved the quality and readability of the eBook. We would also like to acknowledge all the Bentham team and especially Salma Sarfaraz for the help and support.

CONFLICT OF INTEREST

The authors confirm that this eBook content has no conflict of interest.

Seifedine Kadry
School of Engineering
American university of the Middle East
Kuwait

&

Mohammed Z. Al-Taie
Computer Science Department
Al-Salam University College in Baghdad
Iraq

List of Abbreviations

3D	Three Dimensions
API	Application Program Interface
ASCII	American Standard Code for Information Interchange
BASIC	Beginner's All-Purpose Symbolic Instruction Code
CBF	Content-Based Filtering
CF	Collaborative Filtering
DBLP	Digital Bibliography and Library Project
DOS	Disc Operating System
GUI	Graphical User Interface
HIV	Human Immunodeficiency Virus
HRD	Human Resource Development
IMDb	Internet Movie Database
INSNA	International Network for Social Network Analysis
ISBN	International Standard Book Number
JVM	Java Virtual Machine
MS	Microsoft
OpenGL	Open Graphics Library
OS	Operating System

OSN	Online Social Network
OSS	Open Source Software
OWL	Ontology Web Language
RDF	Resource Description Framework
RS	Recommender Systems
SMS	Short Message Service
SN	Social Networks
SNA	Social Network Analysis
SPARQL	Protocol and RDF Query Language
STD	Sexually Transmitted Diseases
WWW	World Wide Web

Send Orders for Reprints to reprints@benthamscience.net

CHAPTER 1

Social Networks and Social Network Analysis

Abstract: In this chapter, we will give a brief description to the main types of networks (with emphasis on social networks), structural properties of networks, basic concepts in graph theory, a historical background showing how social network analysis developed over years, the most important measures used in SNA and finally examples for SNA modeling tools that are used today by researchers of the field.

Keywords: Social networks, social network analysis, graph theory, modeling tools, Blogs, Wiki, Web 2.0, Information networks, Technological networks, UCINET, Pajek, Density, Vertices, Mixing patterns, Degree distribution, Biological networks.

✿ the Web is more a social creation than a technical one. ✿ Tim Berners-Lee

The last decade has witnessed a fast development and a change in the Web and Internet. The accomplishments that have been achieved in computing and communication are drawing people in innovative ways. Huge participatory Web and social sites have emerged, empowering new shapes of collaboration communication. Sites, such as Twitter, Facebook, LinkedIn and MySpace allow people to make new virtual relationships through their online membership. Tremendous numbers of volunteers write articles in scopes and scales considered impossible in the years before. Wikis, Blogs and video Blogs grant Web users the convenience and environment to publish their ideas and thoughts with no need to be worried about the cost of publishing. Online marketplace, such as eBay and Amazon, recommend products to their visitors after investigating their behavior and interaction. Tagging enables Web users to express their perspectives on how the Web should be organized. In addition, the Web also provides the infrastructure for people to publish information and link-related resources with each other using hyperlinks. Each reply to an email, a link to a Web page, or posting of a blog or a comment leaves a digital trace that connects the poster to another online participant. Even political movements are also using the Web to create new forms of collaborative work. All these developments wouldn't take place without the help of Web 2.0, a term coined by O'Reilly, which indicates that individuals are

Seifedine Kadry and Mohammed Z. Al-Taie

now more able to form Web contents. Social networking plays an important role with these interactions, since most Internet users are players of social sites and use them actively and regularly. Inside the social Web, human-to-human interaction is moving further and further towards online communication possibilities. The online communication data are saved and can be computed to large-scale social networks. Recent studies have showed that social networking has become one of three popular usages of the Internet, along-side with the Internet search and e-mail which reflects the growth of this tendency and its significance in communities. Within social networks domain, Social Network Analysis (SNA) makes an interesting interdisciplinary research area, where computer scientists and sociologists bring their competence together. Computer scientists have the knowledge to parse and process the data needed for the Web, while sociologists own specific knowledge necessary for accurate editing and right interpreting of empirical data in their research fields. SNA is used in communication, specifically in economical context and relationship networks.

1.1. TYPES OF NETWORKS

Networks in the real world can be divided into four main types (Newman, 2010, P. 20):

- *Social Networks*: Networks in which the vertices represent people, or groups of people, and the edges represent some form of social interaction between them, such as friendship. We will give detailed description for social networks in the next sections.

- *Information Networks*: These are man-made networks consisting of items of data linked together in some way. The best known example is the World Wide Web (WWW). The WWW is a network in which the vertices are Web pages consisting of text, pictures, or other information. Users can navigate from one page to another through the use of hyperlinks, which are the edges connecting between vertices (Fig. **1**). Other examples of information networks -even though having social aspects to them- include: networks of email communications, networks on social-networking websites such as Facebook MySpace, and networks of weblogs and citation networks.

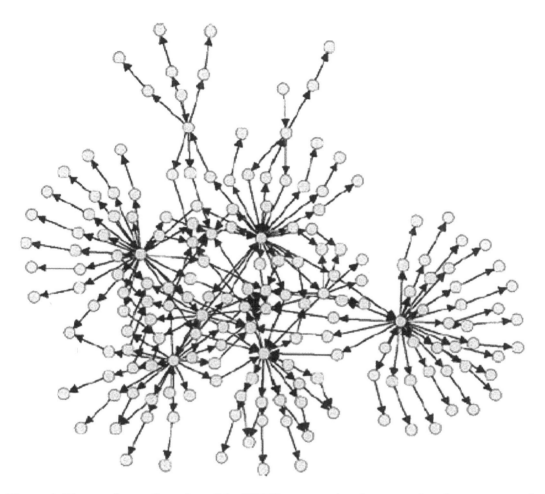

Figure 1: Picture of a small portion of the WWW, representing the connections between a set of Web pages on a single website. (Source: Newman, 2010, p.51).

- *Technological Networks*: Man-made networks that are designed for distribution of commodity or resources. They have grown up over the last century or so and form the backbone of modern technological societies. The most celebrated example is the Internet which is the global network of data connections, electrical, optical, and wireless, that links computers and other information systems together (Fig. **2**). Other examples of technological networks include power grids, transportation networks, delivery and distribution networks, and telephone networks.

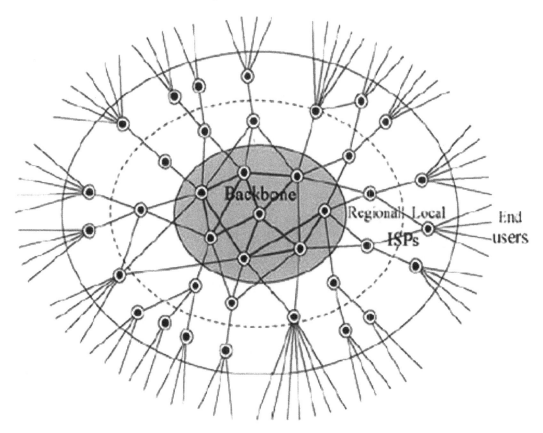

Figure 2: A schematic depiction of the structure of the Internet. (Source: Newman, 2010, p.20).

- *Biological Networks*: Networks that represent patterns of interaction between biological elements. They are widely used in many branches of biology. Examples of biological networks include biochemical networks: networks that represent molecular level patterns of interaction and mechanisms of control in the biological cell, neural networks: networks that exist in the human brain and the central nervous systems in animals and ecological networks: networks of ecological interactions between species.

1.2. STRUCTURAL PROPERTIES OF NETWORKS

The networks mentioned above can be characterized by a number of common features, such as:

- *The Small-World Effect*: a phenomenon described by Stanley Milgram in 1960s which means that most pairs of nodes in most networks seem to be connected by a short path.

- *Transitivity*: also called clustering, which means that if node A is connected to node B, and node B is connected to node C, then there is a high likelihood that node A is also connected to node C.

- *Degree Distribution P(k)*: the probability that a node of a network, chosen uniformly at random, has degree *k*. The degree of vertices can be represented as a histogram, and the distribution of node degrees has a long right tail of values that are far above the mean.

- *Network Resilience*: means that a network is susceptible to vertex removal and that networks vary in their level of resilience to vertex removal. It is one of the simplest indicators of network robustness under a damage done due to node or link removal.

- *Mixing Patterns*: means which vertices pair up with which. In social systems (*e.g.* actor network, company directors, co-authorship networks, phone calls, email address books), links between people who are alike are more common. For example: popular people are connected with popular people. This phenomenon is known as "assortative mixing". However, measurements on the technological and biological systems show that in these systems small degree nodes are more likely to connect to high degree nodes, a phenomenon known as "disassortative mixing".

- *Degree Correlation*: it is a special case of mixing patterns in that it measures how vertices pair up based on their vertex degree.

- *Community Structure*: means that groups of vertices have high density of edges among them however; low density of edges exists between groups. Community structure is an intuitive feature of some networks such as social systems, biological networks, the World Wide Web, co-authorship networks, *etc.* Defining and finding network communities has its history in both sociology and computer science, and has been revisited many times. Finally.

- *Network Navigation*: means that networks not only show the small-world phenomenon but also demonstrate that people are good at finding paths in the network (Newman, 2010, p. 15 and Regan, E., 2009).

Other properties have been noticed in large networks (large networks are defined as having thousands, hundreds of thousands or even millions of vertices) (Goldenberg, 2007, p. 9):

- Groups of acquaintances and friends form cliques (maximum connected components) where everyone knows everyone else.

- Node degree tends to show a power law distribution, which represents the probability that a random node has a certain number of edges.

1.3. GRAPH THEORY

The first article, on graph theory, appeared in 1736 by Leonhard Euler. He considered the problem of the seven bridges of town Konigsberg (now known as Kaliningrad) (Fig. **3**). The problem was how to find a way around Kaliningrad so that his friend, Kant, would not need to repeat the same seven bridges that he took at the beginning of his walk. This problem has led to a new branch of mathematics, namely Graph Theory. He found that his problem had no solution and that they needed an eighth bridge to be erected.

Since social network analysis derives its basic concepts from mathematical graph theory (De Nooy *et al.*, 2005), we are going to spend some time illustrating the main concepts in graph theory (Al-Taie, M. and Kadry, S., 2012):

Simply, a graph is a set of points and lines connecting some pairs of the points. Points are called 'vertices', and lines are called 'edges'. A graph G is a set X of vertices together with a set E of edges and it is written as: $G = (X, E)$. Another way to describe a graph is by giving just the list of all of its edges. For graph G, the edge list, denoted by $J(G)$ is the following:

$$J(G) = \{\{x_1, x_2\}, \{x_2, x_3\}, \{x_3, x_4\},$$

$$\{x_4, x_5\}, \{x_1, x_5\}, \{x_2, x_5\}, \{x_2, x_4\}\}.$$

For a given vertex (x), the number of all vertices adjacent to it is called 'degree' of the vertex x, denoted by $d(x)$. The maximum degree over all vertices is called the maximum degree of G, denoted by Δ (G). The adjacent vertices are sometimes called neighbors of each other, and all the neighbors of a given vertex x are called the neighborhood of x. The neighborhood of x is denoted by $N(x)$. The set of edges incident to a vertex x is denoted by $E(x)$. A cut-vertex (or cutpoint) is a vertex whose removal increases the number of components. A cut-edge is an edge whose removal increases the number of components.

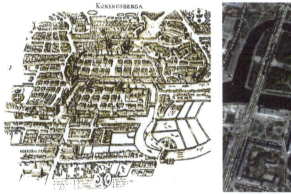 

Figure 3: The Seven Bridges of Königsberg—a 17th century engraving (Left) and The Five Bridges of Kaliningrad (the remaining ones after World War II)—a modern view (Right). (Source: Tsvetovat & Kouznetsov, 2011, p. 23, 24).

A loop is an edge connecting a vertex to it-self. If a vertex has no neighbors, *i.e.* its degree is 0, then these vertices are said to be isolated. If there are many edges connecting the same pair of vertices, then these edges are called 'parallel' or 'multiple'. A simple adjacency between vertices occurs when there is exactly one edge between them. Graphs in which order is not important are called 'undirected graphs'. Undirected graphs without loops and multiple edges are called 'simple graphs' or just simply 'graphs'. A graph in which all vertices can be numbered $x_1, x_2, ..., x_n$ in such a way that there is precisely one edge connecting every two consecutive vertices and there are no other edges, is called a 'path', while the number of edges in a path is the 'length'.

A simple adjacency between vertices occurs when there is exactly one edge between them. A graph in which every pair of vertices is an edge, is called 'complete', denoted by K_n whereas usually, n is the number of vertices. It is complete because we can't add any new edge to it and obtain a simple graph. A graph is called 'connected' if in it any two vertices are connected by some path; otherwise it is called 'disconnected'. It means that in a disconnected graph there always exists a pair of vertices having no path connecting them. Any disconnected graph is a union of two or more connected graphs; each such connected graph is then called a 'connected component' of the original graph. A 'cycle' is a connected graph in which every vertex has degree 2. It is denoted by C_n where n is the number of vertices. If we have a graph $G = (X,E)$ and a vertex $x \in X$: The deletion of x from G means removing x from set X and removing from E all edges of G that contain x. However, the deletion of an edge is easier than that of the vertex, as it comprises only removing the edge from the list of edges.

Let $G = (X,E)$ be a graph, $x,y \in X$. The distance from x to y, denoted by $d(x,y)$, is the length of the shortest (x,y)-path. If there is no such path in G, then $d(x,y) = \infty$. In this case, G is disconnected and x and y are in different components. The diameter of G denoted by $diam(G)$ is $\max_{x,y \in X} d(x,y)$, which means it is the distance between the farthest vertices. A graph $G = (X,D)$ is called 'weighted' if each edge $D \in D$ is assigned a positive real number $w(D)$ called the weight of edge (D). In many practical applications, the weight represents a distance, cost, time, capacity, probability, resistance, *etc.* In a graph G, a walk is an alternating sequence of vertices and edges where every edge connects preceding and succeeding vertices in the sequence. It starts at a vertex, ends at a vertex and has the following form: $x_0, e_1, x_1, e_2, ..., e_k, x_k$.

In a graph, an ordered pair of vertices is called an 'arc'. If (x,y) is an arc, then x is called the initial vertex and y is called the terminal vertex. A graph in which all edges are ordered pairs is called the 'directed graph', or 'digraph'. A digraph $N = (X,A)$ is called a 'network', if X is a set of vertices (also called nodes), A is a set of arcs, and to each arc $a \in A$ a non-negative real number $c(a)$ is assigned which is called the capacity of arc a. For any vertex $y \in X$, any arc of type (x,y) is called 'incoming, and every arc of type (y, z) is called outcoming. A digraph is (weakly) connected if its underlying graph is connected. A digraph is strongly connected if from each vertex to each other vertex there is a directed walk.

Vertices (Nodes): A vertex (or node) is the fundamental unit out of which graphs are formed. An undirected graph (a graph with edges having no direction) consists of a set of vertices and a set of edges (unordered pairs of vertices), while a directed graph (a graph with edges having direction) consists of a set of vertices and a set of arcs (ordered pairs of vertices). Vertices can be distinguished by the following properties (Social Network, 2011, p. 88):

- The *degree* of a vertex in a graph is the number of edges incident to it. An *isolated vertex* is a vertex with degree zero; that is, a vertex that is not an endpoint of any edge. A *leaf vertex* is a vertex with degree one.

- The two vertices forming an edge are said to be its *endpoints*, and the edge is said to be incident to the vertices.

- In a directed graph, the *outdegree* represents number of outgoing edges, while the *indegree* represents the number of incoming edges; a *source vertex* is a vertex with indegree zero, while a *sink vertex* is a vertex with outdegree zero.

- A *cut vertex* is a vertex the removal of which would disconnect the remaining graph while a *vertex separator* is a collection of vertices the removal of which would disconnect the remaining graph into small parts.

- A *k-vertex-connected* graph is a graph in which removing fewer than *k* vertices will not leave the graph disconnected.

- A *labeled vertex* is a vertex that is associated with extra information that enables it to be distinguished from other labeled vertices. An *unlabeled vertex* is one that can be substituted from any other vertex based only on its adjacencies in the graph.

- Two graphs can be considered *isomorphic* only if the correspondence between their vertices pairs up vertices with equal labels.

1.4. SOCIAL NETWORKS

A social network (SN) is a social composition of individuals or organizations that are called "nodes". These nodes are connected through one (or more) type of relationship such as kinship, friendship, knowledge, *etc*. We can consider a SN as a map of ties between investigated nodes. Each individual may be connected to one or more individuals, a structure that represents the social contacts for that individual (Social Network, 2011, p. 1).

These nodes are mostly persons or organizations. However, they could also be Web pages, journal articles, departments, neighborhoods and even countries (Marin & Wellman, 2009). The recent interest in social networks comes from the theoretical and research questions associated with SN and the challenging problems related to data collecting and network analysis (Duijn & Vermunt, 2006).

Ties connecting pairs of actors could be directed (indicating the source and destination of a relationship) or undirected (indicating a reciprocated relationship). They could be dichotomous (to indicate the presence or absence of the relationship) or could be valued (measured on a specific scale) (Borgatti & Foster, 2003).

SN can be classified into two types: one-mode and two-mode networks: One-mode networks are those that consist of actors (usually people), subgroups (people) or communities. The relations among actors in these networks can represent individual evaluation (such as friendship), transfer of materials (such as borrowing or buying), transferring of non-materials (such as communication), interactions, formal roles or kinship (such as marriage). On the other hand, two-mode networks consist of two sets of actors, or one set of actors and one set of events (Wasserman & Faust, 1994, p. 35).

Most of networks are one-mode but, some certain problems require the analysis of two kinds of nodes (such as organizations and organization members, or events and people attending the event) which requires the analysis of two-mode networks (Marin & Wellman, 2009). In the second part of this book, we will learn how to perform both types of analysis.

Network analysts either examine a complete network (which is called socio-centric analysis) or just focusing on the network surrounding a specific one node (which is called ego-centric network analysis) (Fig. **4**).

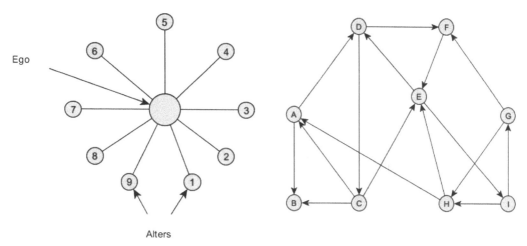

Figure 4: Ego-centric network (Left) and socio-centric network (Right).

Ego-centric network data can be taken from a socio-centric network through selecting one node and examining its neighbors and the connections among them (Marin & Wellman, 2009). One most important property of social networks data is that they are grounded in cultural values and symbols, and are constituted through motives, meanings and typifications.

We can identify three types of SN data (Fig. **5**): 'Relational data', which are the data that emerge from individual's set of direct links such as reachability and reciprocity. 'Attribute data' are those relevant to attributes, opinions and behavior of actors such as items collected through surveys and interviews (Scott, 2000, p. 3; Valente, 2010, p. 55-56). The last type of social network data is the 'Identical data' which describes definitions, motives and meanings. However, analysis techniques of identical data are less well developed than those for the other two types (Scott, 2000, p. 3).

1.5. SOCIAL NETWORK ANALYSIS

Social network analysis (SNA) displays social relationships as consisting of nodes (individuals or organizations) and ties (which are also called links or edges). These nodes represent actors within the SN, and ties represent the relationships between them.

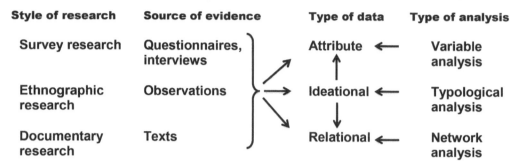

Figure 5: Types of network data analysis. (Source: Scott, 2000, p. 3).

Historical Development: Social Network Analysis has evolved due to the synergy of three fused (and sometimes separated) strands. These strands formalized from the efforts of sociometric analysts who worked on small groups and came up with technical advances in methods of graph theory, the Harvard researchers of the 1930s who discovered patterns of interpersonal relations and the formation of cliques, and the Manchester anthropologists who investigated the structure of community relations in tribal and village societies (Scott, 2000, p. 2).

The roots of SNA go back to Jacob Moreno who, in 1934, put his famous publication "*who shall survive?*" which was a turning point for the development of the field, in addition to important contributions to social network theory and research presented by a group of researchers at Harvard University in the 1970s (Freeman, 2004, p. 6-7).

SNA was developed, initially, in a non-technical schema based on the structural studies of the famous anthropologist Radcliffe-Brown. During the period from 1930s to the 1970s, an increasing number of researchers began to build on his concepts of social structure (Scott, 2000, p.4).

Many scientists, such as Stephen Borgatti, Kathleen Carely, Linton Freeman, Stanley Wasserman and Harrison White have contributed to the expansion of using a systematic SNA (Social Network, 2011, p. 2).

Four features, collectively, are found in the current use of SNA:

- SNA is activated by the structural composition of ties that link social actors.

- It is built on systematic empirical givens.

- It depends strongly on the use of graphical images.

- It depends also on the use of computational and mathematical models.

However, it is just recently when these four components integrated into one organized model for research. Before this, social investigators used only one or some of them. SNA is not only defined by these four attributes. Rather, it goes beyond and can be defined by a variety of growing applications (Freeman, 2004, p. 3-5). As soon as the social network community began to identify the generality of SNA structural approach, a number of useful applications for various experimental cases have become available (Freeman, 2004, p. 4).

Otte and Rousseau (2002) have conducted a research to measure the growth of SNA field for the period (1963-2000). They consulted three databases that related to three branches of science (namely sociology, medicine and psychology). They considered studies only having 'social network analysis' in the 'subject heading' field. In sociology, they retrieved 1601 articles. In medicine, they retrieved 308 articles and in psychology, they retrieved 105 articles. Their results showed that the real growth of the field began in 1981 and there was no sign of decline. The results also show that the development in the field began in sociology faster, while in medicine and psychology it just began later. They mentioned that the success that SNA has witnessed in the eighties was due to the institutionalization of social network analysis since late seventies and the recent availability of textbooks and computer software (Fig. **6**).

Freeman (2004) argues that there has been almost a linear growth in the number of fields in which SNA has contributed (Fig. **7**).

Today, SN analysts have an international organization called *The International Network for Social Network Analysis* or INSNA, which holds annual meetings and issues a number of professional journals. Also, a number of centers for network searching and training have opened worldwide (Freeman, 2004, p. 6-7).

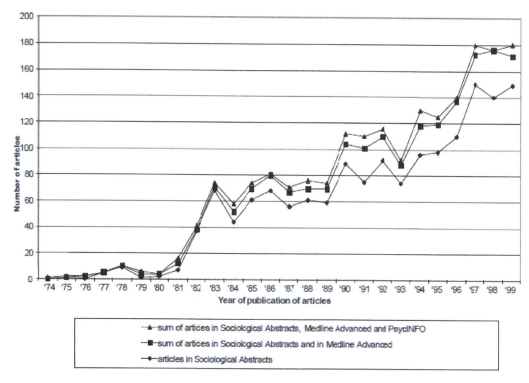

Figure 6: Gowth of social network analysis (values multiplied by 10). (Source: Otte & Rousseau, 2002, p. 13).

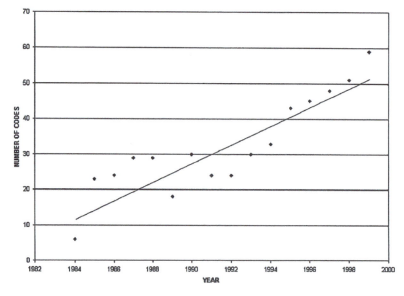

Figure 7: Association between numbers of substantive areas (Source: Freeman, 2004, p. 5).

SNA is an approach in social research that shows four properties: a systematic relational data, structural intuition, graphics and mathematical models (Freeman, 2004, p. 10). It considers the fact 'that social life consists primarily of relations and patterns formed by these relations' as the starting point to its methodology. It is a science in which people influence each other in a way that leads to build the body of knowledge (Freeman, 2004, p. 6).

SNA studies the behavior of the individual (*e.g.* person or organization) at both the micro and macro levels and the interactions between the two (Stockman, 2004).

SNA has risen to be a key technique and has been given a great deal of interest in computer science, economics, anthropology, biology, *etc.*, and has become a popular subject for investigation. SNA has evolved from just being a proposed metaphor to an analytic tool, and finally to a paradigm, which has its researchers, analytic software, concepts and methods.

The essential goal of SNA is to examine relationships among individuals, such as influence, communication, advice, friendship, trust *etc.* Researchers are interested in the evolution of these relationships and the overall structure, in addition to their influence on both individual behavior and group performance (Stockman, 2004).

We can recognize some analytic features that characterize SNA from other types of analysis (Social Network, 2011, p. 2-3):

- It's not the individuals themselves are under investigation. Instead, the structure of ties that affect those individuals and their relationships is the focus of study.

- SNA seeks to find how far the structure and composition of ties can affect norms, rather than looking at socialism into norms as the controller of behavior.

- SNA does not adopt the idea of groups being the building blocks of society. The horizon is open to investigate less-bounded social communications, from non-local communications to links among websites.

Marin and Wellman (2009) see that network analysts not only collect data but also try to analyze them in a way different from that adopted by other social sciences.

However; SNA suffers from a couple of challenges in implementation, such as the use of SNA in education evaluation (Penuel, Sussex, Korbak & Hoadly, 2006), trust and privacy concerns related to SN and ethical and strategic issues in organizational SNA (Borgatti & Molina, 2003).

1.6. SNA METRICS FOR COMPLETE SOCIAL NETWORKS

Metrics that are used with social networks fall into two types: some give information about the position of individuals and how they interact, while others provide information about the global structure of SN:

1.6.1. Density

The number of edges of the network expressed as a proportion of the maximum possible number of edges in that network. Its value is between 0 and 1. For undirected graph, density can be calculated as follows (Bakk, 2010, p. 35):

$$Density_D = \frac{|E|}{|V| * (|V| - 1)}$$

However, for directed networks, the measure can be applied in this way:

$$Density_U = \frac{2\,|E|}{|V| * (|V| - 1)}$$

According to Scott (2000), this measure can be used in the context of egocentric or a socio-centric analysis as follows:

- The ego-centric analysis calculates the density of links around a specific node. Such analysis shows the influence of the analyzed node on the density sub-graph it belongs to with its neighbors.

- The socio-centric analysis calculates the density of a complete graph and also measures the constraint of the network on its members.

The importance of calculating the density of a network is that it gives us a view on some phenomena such as the speed at which information diffuses among nodes, and the extent to which individuals have high levels of social capital or social constraint (Hanneman & Riddle, 2005, p. 99).

1.6.2. Identifying Important Individuals in the Network

Individuals experiencing fewer constraints, and having more chances than others, are in favorable structural positions. Having a favored position means that an individual may practice better bargains in exchanges, have greater effect, and that individual will be a focus for deference and attention from individuals in less favored positions (Hanneman & Riddle, 2005, p. 145). We will apply these measures in the second part of this book.

In order to know who the important players in a network are, we have to use some specific measures. For directed networks the measures are called prestige (also known as Proximity or PageRank). For undirected networks, these measures used are called centrality (degree, closeness or betweenness centrality) (Xu *et al.*, 2009).

1) Degree Centrality: Degree centrality considers nodes with the highest degrees (number of adjacent edges) as the most central. For undirected networks, degree centrality of a specific node is defined as the number of links this node has. A node i's degree centrality d (i) can be formulated as:

$$d(i) = \sum_{j} m_{ij}$$

Where $m_{ij} = 1$ if there is a link between nodes i and j, and $m_{ij} = 0$ if there is no such link. For directed networks, it is important to differentiate between the in-degree centrality and the out-degree centrality.

Identifying individuals with top degree centrality is crucial in the network analysis because actors with many ties means having alternative ways to satisfy needs, and hence are less dependent on other individuals. Also, it means having access to, and be more able to call on the resources of the network as a whole. Users having more ties means they are often third-parties and deal makers in exchanges among others, and are able to benefit from this brokerage (Hanneman & Riddle, 2005, p. 147).

2) Closeness Centrality: Closeness centrality puts into consideration, as most central ones, the vertices that have the smallest average length of the roads (sequence of relationships) linking an actor to other actors. As a mathematical formula of node i's closeness centrality, C(i) can be calculated as follows:

$$C(i) = \sum_j d_{ij}$$

Where d_{ij} is the geodesic distance from node i to node j (the number of links in a shortest path from node i to node j). Closeness centrality is considered an inverse measure of centrality in the way that a larger value indicates a less central node while a smaller value indicates a more central node, because closeness centrality is based on distance between nodes.

Closeness centrality is important because it takes into account not only the immediate ties that an actor has (which is the case of degree centrality measure), but also indirect ties to all other nodes in the network (Hanneman & Riddle, 2005, p. 154).

3) Betweenness Centrality: Betweenness centrality of a node (i) is defined as the number of shortest paths between pairs of nodes that run through (i). The betweenness centrality of nodes i can be obtained *via* the following formula:

$$b(i) = \sum_{j,k} \frac{g_{jik}}{g_{jk}}$$

Where g_{jk} is the number of shortest paths from node (j) to node k (j and k $\neq$ i), and g_{jik} is the number of shortest paths from node (j) to node k passing through node (i).

The more people depend on a person to make connections with other people, the more power that person has (high betweenness centrality value). If, however, two people are connected by more than one geodesic path, and the person was not on any of them, that person will lose some power (low betweenness centrality value) (Hanneman & Riddle, 2005, p. 163).

1.6.3. Cohesive Subgroups

The distribution of degree of a single vertex doesn't tell us whether a vertex with high degree is clustered (connected to other vertices) or scattered over the network. In this case, we me pay attention to the degree of all vertices within a cluster.

Subgroups indicate areas of density within the network so; they are more found in undirected networks than in their equivalent directed networks because density within undirected network is higher than that of the other type.

Several techniques have been devised to detect cohesive subgroups within a network such as k-core (a sub-network in which each vertex is connected with at least k within the sub-network), cliques (maximal connected component, usually consist of 3 vertices) and m-slice, in addition to other techniques. However, all of them share the same concepts of density and connectedness (De Nooy *et al.*, 2005, p. 77).

The importance of identifying cohesive subgroups is that they point out to a potential social clustering within the network (Cheng, 2006, p. 86).

1.6.4. M-Slice

It is a maximal sub-network containing the lines with a multiplicity equal to (or greater) than m and the vertices incident with these lines. It helps to define cohesive subgroups depending on line multiplicity. This concept was first introduced by John Scott as 'm-core'. Isolated nodes are defined (according to this concept) as 0-slice, since they share nothing among them. However, m-slice does not guarantee that all vertices within the m-slice component are connected at a minimum level of line-multiplicity. Instead, components within m-slice are considered as cohesive subgroups, rather than the m-slice itself (De Nooy *et al.*, 2005, p. 109-110).

1.6.5. Brokerage Roles

A brokerage role of a vertex is a specific pattern of links and group affiliations (De Nooy *et al.*, 2005, p. 318). This concept examines ego's relations with its neighborhood from the perspective of ego acting as an agent in relations among groups. To inspect the brokerage roles played by an actor in a network, we find every instance where that actor lies on the directed path between two other actors. So, each actor may have many opportunities to act as a broker (Hanneman & Riddle, 2005, p. 139).

1.6.6. Components/Isolates

A component exits if a set of actors are connected within each other but at the same time they are disconnected from the reset of vertices in the network. When a vertex is isolated from other vertices, then simply it becomes *isolate* (Cheng, 2005, p. 89).

1.6.7. Core/Periphery

In a core, members are densely tied, however, in a periphery they are more tied to the core members than to each other (Cheng, 2005, p. 88).

For example, De Nooy, Mrvar and Batagelj (2005) presented the economic world system in 1974 as an instance for the use of core and periphery, where countries in the middle of the model (the core countries) are the wealthy countries, represented by USA, Japan and the western countries, while countries in the periphery of the model represent the poor countries (such as Bolivia, Panama and Nicaragua). However, another sphere of countries called semi-periphery intermediate the communication between the core and periphery.

Hanneman & Riddle (2005) argue that actors with many ties (at the core of a network) and actors with only few ties (at the periphery of a network) have constrained and predictable behavioral patterns, as compared to actors with only some ties, whose behavior is not predictable and depends mainly on whom they are connected.

1.6.8. Structural Holes

There is a structural hole in the ego-network of a vertex if two of its neighbors are not connected directly (De Nooy *et al.*, 2005, p. 345-353). The concept was coined by Ronald Burt to refer to some important aspects of positional advantage/disadvantage of actors that result from how they are embedded in a network. Burt's establishment of these ideas, and his development to a number of metrics have paved the way to a great deal of further thinking about how and why, the ways in which actors are connected, affect their constraints and opportunities and consequently their behavior (Hanneman & Riddle, 2005, p. 136).

1.7. OTHER NETWORK MEASURES

In addition to the above measures, there are also other ones that we want to talk about, here, with some brief (De Nooy *et al.*, 2005, p. 345-353; Hanneman & Riddle, 2005, p. 135):

- Aggregate Constraint: The aggregate constraint on a vertex is the sum of the dyadic constraint on all of its ties.

- Average Degree: It is used to measure the structural cohesion of a network. To calculate the average degree: all degrees are summed and then divided by the total number of nodes in the network.

- Average Geodesic Distance: It is the mean of the shortest path lengths among all connected pairs in the ego network.

- Betweenness Centralization: The variation in the betweenness centrality of vertices divided by the maximum variation in betweenness centrality scores possible in a similar network.

- Closeness Centralization: It is the variation in the closeness centrality of vertices divided by the maximum variation in closeness centrality scores possible in a network of the same size.

- Clustering Coefficient: How likely two associates of a node are associates.

- Degree Centralization: It is the variation in the degrees of vertices divided by the maximum degree variation which is possible in a similar network.

- Diameter: It is the longest shortest path in the network. The idea behind the network diameter is to index the extensiveness of the network, namely how far apart are the two furthest nodes.

- Dyad: A dyad is a pair of nodes and the lines between them.

- Dyadic Constraint: The dyadic constraint on vertex u exercised by a tie between vertices u and v is the extent to which u has more and stronger ties with neighbors that are strongly connected with vertex v.

- Event: It is a happening, context, or organization where actors may gather.

- Geodesic: Is the shortest path between two vertices.

- Multiple Lines: If a particular arc or edge occurs more than once, there are multiple lines.

- Multiplicity: It is the number of times a specific line (ordered or unordered pair of vertices) occurs in a network.

- Popularity: The popularity of a vertex is the number of arcs it receives in a directed network.

- Rate of Participation: In a 2-mode network, the degree of a node is called the rate of participation of an actor if the node refers to an actor.

- Size of an Event: In a 2-mode network, the degree of a vertex is known as the size of an event if that vertex refers to an event.

- Star-Network: It is a network in which one vertex is connected to all vertices, but these vertices are not connected among themselves.

- Triad: A triad is a sub-network consisting of three nodes.

- Weak Components: A weak component is the maximum number of actors who are connected, disregarding the direction of the ties, while a strong component pays attention to the direction of the ties.

1.8. SNA MODELING TOOLS

To identify, represent, analyze or visualize nodes and edges in a social network, SNA employs a number of specialized tools. These tools help researchers study networks of different sizes and different properties. Visual representation, which most new modeling tool support, help to better understanding the network, since visualization tools can be used to change size, colors, layout and other attributes. The output of SN representation can be saved or exported to various file formats (Social Network, 2011, p. 12).

SNA software facilitates the job of quantitative or qualitative analysis of SN. This is done through describing network features either graphically or numerically. The job of these programs is to convert the node-list or link-list (*i.e.* the data saved in database) to the corresponding matrix or graph displays (Valente, 2010, p. 51).

It is possible, in some cases, to use spreadsheet programs (such as MS Excel) if a suitable SNA tool was not available, along with word processor (such as MS Word) (Scott, 2000, p. 50).

SNA modeling tools fall (according to software availability) into two types: commercial and free packages.

They can be also classified into stand-alone programs (such as UCINET) and utility tool kits (such as NodeXL) (Carrington, Scott & Wasserman, 2005, p. 270), or be classified into packages with scripting/programming utility, such as JUNG and SNAP-GAUSS, and those with graphical user interface (GUI), such as Pajek or UCINET (Carrington *et al.*, 2005, p. 309). Tools with a GUI are easy to learn, while those provided with only scripting utilities are more powerful and come with extensible jobs.

The number of new SNA tools is increasing, since everyday new applications are emerging so, the total number is not confirmed by all researchers. Scott (2000) gave details for only four packages, which he considered the major ones at his time, in addition to a brief introduction to other three packages. Carrington *et al.* (2005) have deeply analyzed twenty-seven software packages, while Social Network (2011) presented a brief description to about fifty five software packages. INSNA, in its official website, maintains a long list of all packages and libraries.

1.9. EXAMPLES OF SNA TOOLS

Social network analysis tools are used to identify, represent, analyze, visualize, or simulate nodes and edges from various types of input data. These tools allow researchers to investigate representations of networks of different size - from small (*e.g.* families, project teams) to very large (*e.g.* the Internet, disease transmission). The various tools provide mathematical and statistical routines that can be applied to the network model.

1.10. GENERAL-PURPOSE PACKAGES

These are comprehensive general-purpose programs for the analysis of social networks and other proximity data:

1.10.1. UCINET

UCINET can deal with both types of networks: 1-mode and 2-mode networks. A number of SNA metrics can be applied through the use of UCINET such as: centrality measures (degree centrality, betweenness centrality and closeness centrality), subgroup identification, role analysis, elementary and graph theory. In addition, the package has strong matrix analysis routines.

It is a comprehensive tool for the analysis of social network. It is probably the most well-known software package, containing a large number of network analytic routines, with a menu-driven window. This program is commercial, although a trial version for 30 days is available (Carrington *et al.*, 2005, p. 275).

UCINET was produced basically by a group of network analysts at the University of California, Irvine (this is where the name comes from), began as a set of modules written in BASIC programming language. Later on, it was developed to run on DOS environment, and then on Windows (Scott, 2000, p. 178).

UCINET accepts data from Excel, Pajek, text, *etc.* The package has strong matrix analysis procedures such as matrix algebra and multivariate statistics (Social Network, 2011, p. 36).

UCINET is good in terms of availability of manuals, online help and user friendliness. It is very good in terms of data manipulation, descriptive methods and procedure-based methods. However; it has good and bad parts in terms of statistical methods (Carrington *et al*. 2005, p. 311).

1.10.2. Pajek

The software that we use in this book in network analysis is specifically *Pajek*, a program for analysis and visualization of large networks (Batagelj & Mrvar, 2003) (Fig. **8**). It can be used to calculate most centrality measures, identify structural holes, block-model *etc.* and to analyze both one-mode and two-mode networks (Social Network, 2011, p. 29).

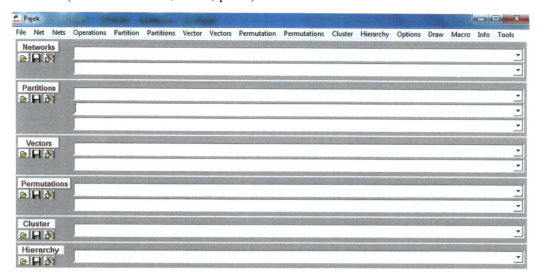

Figure 8: Pajek, a specialized SNA software.

Several reasons were behind choosing this software (with the availability of many other free software packages). Pajek is capable of dealing with large networks (several hundred thousand and even millions of nodes), a task not every program can handle successfully. It is freely available to download from the Internet. It has a simple GUI, which gives the chance to machine resources to function easily and efficiently. It has a well-illustrated user's manual and a lot of free compatible datasets for testing purposes. It has powerful visualization tools and several data analytic algorithms. Also, it has the ability to deal with different types of networks (1, 2-mode networks, static and temporal networks) and many networks at the same time. Also, Pajek has the ability to integrate with very powerful statistical analysis tools (R and SPSS) (Batagelj & Mrvar, 2003). The version that was use in this book is "2.05".

Pajek File Formats: Pajek can read data files containing unformatted text (ASCII). One of the most famous file format used in this context is the Pajek Network Format (files with extensions.net) (Fig. **9**). The file is merely a list of vertices followed by a list of edges and arcs. Nodes have basically one unique identifier and a label. The definition of nodes starts with the chain *vertices N where *N* is the number of nodes following. Edges are either defined as list of nodes identifier or pair of two nodes: for the first case; edges are defined as pair of nodes identifier while the *arcs* marker goes before the pairs list. Weight is added by a third column. It is the most flexible format since it allows for multiple lines. Also, we can specify many layout properties for lines and arcs. There are three network file formats: Arcs-Edges, ArcsList-EdgsList and ArcsList-EdgesList.

```
*Vertices 26
1 "Ada" 0.1646 0.1077 0.5000
2 "Cora" 0.0481 0.3446 0.5000
3 "Louise" 0.3472 0.0759 0.5000
[...]
25 "Laura" 0.5101 0.6557 0.5000
26 "Irene" 0.7478 0.9241 0.5000
*Arcs
1 3 2
1 2 1
2 1 1
[...]
25 15 1
25 17 2
26 13 1
26 24 2
*Edges
```

Figure 9: Pajek (.net) file format.

The other type of file formats, largely used within Pajek, is the Pajek Matrix format (files with extensions.mat) (Fig. **10**). This is similar to the (.net) format in that the list of vertices is the same but the list of edges and arcs is replaced by a matrix of integers or real numbers separated by spaces. The Pajek matrix format is very useful for importing network data in matrix format from a variety of sources.

```
*Vertices 6
1 "Ada" 0.1646 0.2144 0.5000
2 "Cora" 0.0481 0.3869 0.5000
3 "Louise" 0.3472 0.1913 0.5000
4 "Jean" 0.1063 0.5935 0.5000
5 "Helen" 0.2892 0.6688 0.5000
6 "Martha" 0.4630 0.5179 0.5000
*Matrix
0.000 1.000 1.000 0.000 0.000 0.000
1.000 0.000 0.000 1.000 0.000 0.000
0.000 0.000 0.000 0.000 0.000 0.000
0.000 0.000 0.000 0.000 1.000 0.000
0.000 0.000 0.000 1.000 0.000 0.000
0.000 0.000 0.000 0.000 0.000 0.000
```

Figure 10: Pajek (.mat) file format.

Other file formats that are used within Pajek include Vega (devised by Pisanski), GEDCOM (used with genealogical data), UCINET DL (to import/export data from/to UCINET software package), Ball and Stick, Mac Molecule and MDL. The last three formats were developed for chemistry and not widely used (De Nooy *et al.*, 2005, p. 292-293). For more details, please refer to Pajek manual.

Pajek is of Slovenian origin, means a spider, and was released in 1996. The program runs in Windows environment and displays the results in subsidiary windows (Scott, 2000, p. 179).

Many commands have been embedded within Pajek window in order to control the layout (such as the size, color, spin, *etc.*) in addition to the graphical representation of partitions, vectors and combinations of them (Carrington *et al.*, 2005, p. 282).

Pajek has several procedure-based methods, such as detecting structural balance, clusterability, hierarchical decomposition, *etc.* (Carrington *et al.*, 2005, p. 285).

Nevertheless, Pajek is considered weak in terms of availability of manuals and online help, somewhat good regarding data manipulation and descriptive methods, and with some bad and good parts regarding user friendliness. However; it is strong in terms of network visualization capabilities and procedure-based methods (Carrington *et al.*, 2005, p. 311).

1.10.3. STRUCTURE

STRUCTURE supports network models within five types of network analysis: analysis of structural holes, detection of cliques, analysis of structural or role equivalence and blockmodeling, and power analysis of network prominence and equilibrium (Carrington *et al.*, 2005, p. 292).

It began its life in 1975 by Burt, who tried to use the program to apply his ideas in structural autonomy. The program has no Windows version. Instead, it uses the DOS prompt. It is easy to use but lacks a wide range of graphic display found in other programs (Scott, 2000, p. 177).

According to Carrington *et al.* (2005), the program is free to download from the Internet. It has few data manipulation options which are available only for directed relations. The program does not contain procedures to visualize networks. The procedure-based analysis methods in STRUCTURE are hierarchical clusters analysis and eigenvalue decomposition. It also has two routines for statistical modeling of data: contagion analysis and analysis of network equilibrium.

STRUCTURE shows strong features regarding availability of manuals and the procedure-based methods and it gives good features regarding statistical methods. However, it lacks network visualization and online help (Carrington *et al.*, 2005, p. 311).

1.10.4. StOCNET

The software is used for advanced statistical analysis of social networks. It is an open-source program, can be downloaded for free from the Internet, and works in Windows environment (Carrington *et al.*, 2005, p. 301).

Some of the network statistics that are calculated are: Degree variances, index of heterogeneity, dyad and triad census, degree of reciprocity and transitivity, and segmentation.

It takes a text file as an input (with formats such as.dat and.txt). It focuses mainly on probabilistic models, and the current version of it consists of six modules for network analysis (Social Network, 2011, p. 35).

1.10.5. Gephi

It is an interactive visualization plus exploration software that can be used for all types of networks, complex systems, dynamic and hierarchical graphs. To speed up processing and display large networks in real-time, Gephi uses a 3-D rendering engine. Gephi is considered a suitable tool for people seeking to discover and understand graphs. Drawing palettes allow users to change layout settings while drawing, which in turn increases user experience and feedback (Gephi, 2011). It is an open source program and can run under any OS that supports JVM and openGL. It supports different file formats such as NetworkX, NodeXL, Pajek and UCINET. For output, it can export files with extensions such as.gdf, svg and png (Social Network, 2011, p. 19).

1.10.6. Network Workbench

It is a tool for modeling, analyzing and visualizing large networks. It consists of a variety of algorithms such as PageRank, Pathfinder network scaling and small world network generation. It also allows users to add plugins to the software and thus expands the program's utility. Users of Network Workbench program have online access to major datasets and they can also upload their own datasets. They are able to do network analysis with the most influential algorithms and can validate their network models in order for better understanding of the structure and dynamics of specific networks (Network Workbench, 2011). It accepts files with extensions such as.csv and.net, and can output files with extensions such as.net,.mat,.graphml,.nwb,.csv,.xgmml,.eps and.pdf (Social Network, 2011, p. 26).

1.10.7. Network Overview Discovery Exploration for Excel

Network Overview Discovery Exploration for Excel (NodeXL) is add-in software with C# and.net library for network analysis and exploration. It integrates into the well-known software, namely MS Excel, and calculates a core set of network measures. It has several nice features such as the flexibility of import/export, direct connectivity to social networks, easily adjusted appearance, dynamic filtering, powerful vertex grouping, graph metric calculations and task automation (NodeXL, 2011). It can extract email, Twitter, YouTube and Flick social networks. Free software that for input, it accepts files with extensions such as.csv,.xls, and.net and for output, it can produce files with extensions such as.xslt,.csv and.txt (Social Network, 2011, p. 25).

1.11. SPECIAL-PURPOSE PACKAGES

These are software packages that were designed for specific analysis aims such as identification of subgroups, knowledge networks, hidden populations, kinship networks, and statistical testing:

1.11.1. NEGOPY (Subgroups Identification)

This is one of the original network analysis packages, provided by Bill Richards. It can run on both DOS and Windows platforms (Scott, 2000, p. 180). The main use of NEGOPY is to find cohesive subgroups. To this end, it defines a number of role categories, such as groups, isolates, or participants on the basis of their linkage with other nodes, more or less similar to the p-cliques. To approximate eigendecomposition methods unfeasible for large networks, NEGOPY uses partial decomposition methods (Carrington *et al.*, 2005, p. 308).

1.11.2. InFlow (Visual Exploration)

The most popular network metrics embedded in InFlow include: Density, Geodesics, Centralities, Small World, Structural Equivalence, Cluster Analysis, E/I Ratio, and Weighted Average Path Length.

This commercial software package is for network mapping purposes. Basically, it was presented to work on Macintosh environment Later on, it was developed to work on Windows environment too as it can run on different windows platforms, such as Windows XP and Windows Vista (Carrington *et al.*, 2005, p. 306). It can easily import files from MS office package and.csv files. Several network layouts are possible to generate using automated algorithms and geometric layouts, which results in an unlimited number of custom views (Social Network, 2011, p. 22).

1.11.3. SocioMetric LinkAlyzer (Hidden Populations)

This software is aimed to construct a network from a hidden or difficult population. It can be used for example, to investigate a network of Human Immunodeficiency Virus (HIV) links between drug users, where many nodes are difficult to identify because of the possible use of nicknames. The software is commercial but, a demo version is available (Carrington *et al*., 2005, p. 309). The program can take input files from different other software packages such as MS Excel and UCINET. It runs on Windows environment and provides prototype functionality for analysis by using relational algebra model (Social Network, 2011, p. 32).

1.12. PACKAGES WITH PROGRAMMING UTILITY

Some libraries have been developed in different programming languages for computations on networks. We describe here in brief some of them:

1.12.1. Java Universal Network/Graph

Java Universal Network/Graph (JUNG) is a Java Application Program Interface (API) and library, which presents a common and extensible language for modeling, analysis and visualization of data that can be represented as a graph or a network. It has the ability to analyze networks with more than one million nodes, and is limited only by the amount of memory available (Social Network, 2011, p. 310). JUNG supports directed, undirected graphs and includes algorithms for clustering, decomposition, random graph generation, statistical analysis, and calculating of network distances, flows, and importance measures. It also provides a visualization framework (Carrington *et al*., 2005, p. 310).

1.12.2. iGraph

This software performs different network analysis methods such as community structure search, cohesive blocking, structural holes, dyad and triad census and motif count estimation.

It is used for analysis and visualization of large networks. It contains fast implementation for graph theory problems (such as minimum spanning trees and network flow) and can implement algorithms for recent network analysis methods (such as community structure search). It also includes an interface for programming with C library, R package, Python and Ruby extensions. iGraph is open source software (OSS), runs under different OS such as Windows, Linux and OSx, supports files with extensions such as.txt,.graphml and.net, and can output files with extensions such as.dot and.gml (Social Network, 2011, p. 21).

1.12.3. NetworkX

NetworkX (NX) is software used in the study of the structure, dynamics, and functions of complex networks and is provided with an interface where users can do Python scripting. It is an open source project that started in 2004 with user forums and open bug tracking site, whereas development was sponsored by Los Alamos National Lab. It is free software that accepts file formats such as GML, GraphML and NetworkX, while it can output files with extensions such as .dot, .net, .jpg, .png *etc.* (Social Network, 2011, p. 27).

1.12.4. Prefuse

It is a Java-based software framework that can be used to establish applications for information visualization. It uses 2-D java graphics library and can integrate into Swing applications or Java applets. Prefuse implementation relies on the information visualization reference model which breaks up the visualization process into a series of discrete steps. It is free software and can be used for non-commercial purposes.

1.12.5. Stanford Network Analysis Project

Stanford Network Analysis Project (SNAP) is a general purpose network analysis that is written in (C++) and can straightforward scale to a network with hundreds of millions of nodes. It can efficiently compute structural properties and generate regular and random graphs. It is also available through NodeXL (SNAP, 2011).

1.13. SELECTION OF SNA TOOL

The selection of the program depends on the personal preference, and maybe the domestic budget (Scott, 2000, p. 180). On the other hand, Valente (2010) considered that the selection is related to the type of data used. For egocentric data, statistical packages (such as SPSS) are the choice. If the data were census, then programs such as UCINET, Pajek, Visualizer, *etc.* are suitable for three or fewer networks. However; with many networks, a programming language will be necessary in order to allow repetition of network calculations (Valente, 2010, p. 52).

Carrington *et al.* (2005) have identified six main SNA modeling tools (Multinet, NetMiner, Pajek, StOCNET, STRUCTURE and UCINET) based on functionality (*i.e.* data manipulation, network visualization, descriptive methods, procedure-based methods and statistical methods), support (*i.e.* availability of manuals or on-line help) and user friendliness. The authors also argue that SNA modeling tools have different objectives, which in turn reflects their functionality. For example, StOCNET does not contain procedure-based methods since it runs as an addition to existing software, while STRUCTURE is too old to offer visualization.

Send Orders for Reprints to reprints@benthamscience.net

Social Network Analysis, **2014**, 36-55

CHAPTER 2

Research Design

Abstract: In this chapter, the main phases of research design are exhibited, starting from data sampling techniques (examples include snow ball network sampling and ego-centered sampling), data collection methods (techniques such as questionnaires and interviews *etc.* are discussed), and data visualization (where graphs, trees and matrices are explained in some detail). However, data analysis which is the last step in research design will be addressed, later, in chapter 4.

Keywords: Data sampling, data collection, data visualization, Matrix, Trees, Dijkstra's algorithm, Graph traversals, Binary operations, Directed graph, Undirected graph, Deployed applications, Online social networks, Observation, Interviews, Questionnaires, ego-centered sampling, Maps.

2.1. DATA SAMPLING

In some cases, it would not be possible to take measurements on all actors in the relevant actor set. Therefore; a sample of actors may be taken from the set, and inference made about the populations of actors from the sample. This sampling technique is known as probability sample. One usually views a sample as representative of the larger population and uses the sampled actors and data to make inferences about the population. Various sampling techniques have been devised by different researchers in the last century. One clever idea is called the *Snow Ball Network Sampling*. This idea begins when the actors in a set of sampled respondents report on the actors to whom they have ties. All of these nominated actors constitute the first-order zone of the network. The researcher then will sample all the actors in this zone and gather all the additional actors. These additional actors constitute the second-order zone. This sampling technique proceeds through several zones. There is also what is called *ego-centered sampling* technique where one might sample actors, and have them report on their ties and the ties that might exist among the actors they choose or nominate.

2.2. DATA COLLECTION METHODS IN SOCIAL NETWORKS

There are various types of data collection methods. These collection methods attempt to measure the ties among all the actors in the network. It is not unusual that one study employs a variety of data collection methods, in addition to gathering actor attribute information. For each type of data collection method, data, data management and data analysis are different. Traditionally, a number of techniques have been used in data collection: questionnaires, interviews, observations, archival records, experiments and other techniques (Wasserman & Faust, 1994, p. 43):

- *Questionnaires*: this is the most commonly method used in data collection. They are most useful when the actors are people and the relations that are being studied are the ones that the respondent can report on. A questionnaire usually contains questions about the respondent's ties with the other actors. It can also be used when the actor in a study is a collective entity, such as corporation, but an individual person representing the collective reports on the collective's ties. For example, people can report on who they like, respect or go to for advice. Questionnaires fall into three types of format: Roster *vs.* free call, free *vs.* fixed choice and ratings *vs.* complete rankings.

- *Interviews*: they are used whenever questionnaires are not feasible. They are used to gather network data either face to face, over the telephone or by any other means.

- *Observation*: they include observing interactions among actors to collect network data. This method has been used to study relatively small groups of people who have face-to-face interactions. Observational methods can be used to observe interactions among people in a variety of social settings such as a social science research office, faculty, staff and graduate students in a university department, and members of a college fraternity. They are also widely used in the study of interactions among non-human primates such as monkeys. They can also be useful for collecting affiliation network data, as the researcher can record who attends each of a number of social events.

- *Archival Records*: this method includes measuring ties by examining measurements taken from records of interactions. These records can take the form of past political interactions among nations, previously published citations of one scholar by another, journal articles, newspapers, court records, minutes of meetings and so on. The importance of this method is that such data give rise to longitudinal relations and can be used to reconstruct ties that existed in the past. Another use for archival records is for the study of sociology of science such as patterns of citations among scholars.

- *Other*: other relational data collecting methods include the cognitive social structure design, experimental studies and studies in which information is collected on ties among just some actors. These studies are usually used to estimate the size or composition of an individual's ego-centered network.

In addition to the traditional methods of data collection, data of online nature can be collected through the following ways:

- *Online Social Networks*: as these networks have showed recently to allow Internet users to share their activities, photographs and other content with one another. They contain large quantities of personal information. These data not only provide information on the users themselves, but also describe their social interactions. For example, Facebook stores more than 30 billion pieces of new content each month, shared by over 500 million users. One way to collect data from online social networks (OSN) is to use an API provided by the OSN provider. This way includes sending queries to the OSN with the API to collect data. An alternative method can be used for OSN when the data are not available through APIs. This method includes building a Web crawler to crawl the OSN website using a script that investigate the website and collect the data by using HTTP requests/responses.

- *Surveys*: they include studying users' behavior through asking them how, when, and to whom they would share content.

- *Deployed Applications*: This method consists of deploying a custom application used by participants to share content on OSNs. This method provides more flexibility to monitor users' behavior *in situ*, and the content that participants do not share to their social network can still be collected by the researchers.

Nevertheless; network data collection methods suffer from several shortcomings that are related to information accuracy, information validity, information reliability and measurement error (Wasserman & Faust, 1994, p. 56).

2.3. DATA VISUALIZATION

Data visualization can be an extremely useful tool in the analysis of network data through allowing viewers to see instantly important structural features of a network that would otherwise be difficult to capture with raw data only. Since the human eye is gifted at picking out patterns, visualization techniques allow us to put this gift to work and solve our network problems. Thus, in data visualization, data of big size are aggregated and put in a way that allows for fast communication of rich messages, explore new facts and relationships and acquire a deep insight into things that we may already know. Visualization can be achieved through the following ways:

2.3.1. Graphs

A graph is a structure for modeling information. It consists of nodes that represent objects, and edges that show relationships among nodes. Graph theory offers the tools needed to describe and visualize social compositions that consist of three or more actors. This resulted in a new realization to the social composition as a system of ties that represents both the human action and the context for human action (De Nooy, 2009, p. 3). Freeman (2004) traced back the roots of the first use of visual images to Jacob Moreno (1932-1934) when the latter used these images to show the pattering of linkages among social actors. On the other hand, the use of graph theory on social relations started by a group of mathematicians and psychologists in the 1940s.

Graph theory allows researchers to prove theorems and deduce testable statements. It also gives a representation of a social network as a model of a social system consisting of actors and the ties among them.

Graph theory has been useful in social network analysis for many reasons:

- First, it provides a vocabulary which can be used to label and denote many social structural properties.

- Second, it gives us mathematical operations and ideas with which many of these properties can be quantified and measured.

- Third, graph theory gives us the ability to prove theorems about graphs and representations of social structure.

In a graph of a social network with a single non-directional dichotomous relation, the nodes represent actors and the lines represent the ties that exist between pairs of actors on the relation.

A graph could be in any of the following forms (Social Network, 2011, p. 63; Abraham, Hassanian & Snasel, 2010, p. 11-12 and Maarten, 2010, P. 50):

- *Undirected Graph*: a graph with edges having no direction. These graphs are used to represent symmetric links. For example, if the vertices represent people at a party, and there is an edge between two people if they shake hands, then this is an undirected graph, because if person A shook hands with person B, then person B also shook hands with person A (Fig. **11 -a**). We can transform any undirected graph *G* into a directed one, D(G), by associating a direction with each edge.

- *Directed Graph*: also called digraph, is a graph with edges having directions. To show the importance of directed graphs: in social networks, it is often convenient to represent the fact that Alice knows Bob, but the opposite is not true. This is done by representing people by vertices, and a directed edge is used to represent who knows whom. Another example is in computer networks, and notably wireless networks. Links between two different nodes are often not symmetric as messages can be sent from station A to B, but not the other direction. Modeling such network is more conveniently done using directed edges (Fig. **11 –b**).

- *Weighted Graph*: A weight is a real value associated with an edge. Weights might represent, for example, costs, lengths or capacities, *etc.* depending on the problem. For example, when modeling a railway network as a graph, railway stations are represented by vertices, whereas and edge connects two adjacent stations. Then a weight is assigned to an edge representing the distance between those two stations. The weight of the graph is the sum of the weights assigned to all edges (Fig. **11 -c**).

- *Planar Graph*: a graph with no crossing among ties. Planarity can play an important role. For example, when designing a transportation network, if the corresponding graph is planar, this means that there is no need to use bridges and tunnels. Another example is when designing electrical circuits, such as those for chips. Here, it is important that the wires that connect components do not cross each other. One way is to design chips as a collection of layers, with each layer having an associated planar graph (Fig. **11 –d**).

- *Orthogonal Graph*: a graph with horizontal and vertical lines (Fig. **11 -e**).

- *Grid-based Graph*: a graph in which the vertices and edges are organized as in a two-dimensional grid (Fig. **11 -f**).

Other types of graphs include:

- *Mixed Graph*: A mixed graph *G* is a graph in which some edges may be directed and some may be undirected. Directed and undirected graphs are special cases.

- *Multigraph*: The term "multigraph" is generally understood to mean that multiple edges (and sometimes loops) are allowed.

- *Simple Graph*: a simple graph is an undirected graph that has no loops and no more than one edge between any two different vertices. The edges of the graph form a set (rather than a multiset) and each edge is a pair of distinct vertices.

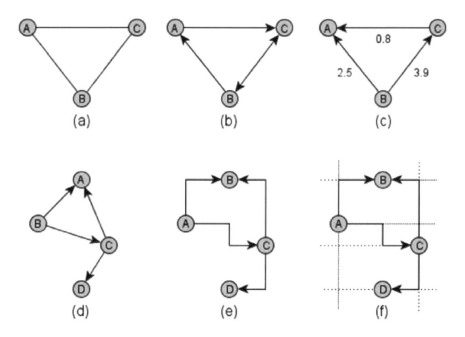

Figure 11: Types of graphs (a) Undirected graph (b) Directed graph (c) Weighted graph (d) Planar graph (e) Orthogonal graph (f) Grid-based graph.

- *Half-Edges, Loose Edges Graph*: it is a graph with only one end, called half-edges, or no ends (loose edges). Examples include: *signed graphs* and *biased graphs*.

- *Regular Graph*: A regular graph is a graph where each vertex has the same number of neighbors, *i.e.*, every vertex has the same degree.

- *Complete Graph*: in complete graphs, each pair of vertices has an edge connecting them.

- *Finite and Infinite Graphs*: A finite graph is a graph $G = (V, E)$ such that V and E are finite sets. An infinite graph is one with an infinite set of vertices or edges or both.

- *Connected and Disconnected Graph*: A graph is called connected if every pair of distinct vertices in the graph is connected; otherwise, it is called disconnected.

- *K-Vertex-Connected Graph*: A graph is called k-vertex-connected or k-edge-connected if no set of k-1 vertices (respectively, edges) exists that disconnects the graph. A k-vertex-connected graph is often called simply k-connected.

- *Weakly and Strongly Connected Graph*: A directed graph is called weakly connected if replacing all of its directed edges with undirected edges produces a connected (undirected) graph. It is strongly connected or strong if it contains a directed path from u to v and a directed path from v to u for every pair of vertices u, v.

Properties of Graphs: All graphs have the following properties (Social Network, 2011, p. 65):

- Two edges of a graph are called adjacent (sometimes coincident) if they share a common vertex. Two arrows of a directed graph are called consecutive if the head of the first one is at the nock (notch end) of the second one.

- Two vertices are called adjacent if they share a common edge (consecutive if they are at the notch and at the head of an arrow), in which case the common edge is said to join the two vertices. An edge and a vertex on that edge are called incident.

- The graph with only one vertex and no edges is called the trivial graph. A graph with only vertices and no edges is known as an edgeless graph. The graph with no vertices and no edges is sometimes called the null graph or empty graph.

- In a weighted graph or digraph, each edge is associated with some value, variously called its cost, weight, length or other term depending on the application.

- Normally, the vertices of a graph, by their nature as elements of a set, are distinguishable. This kind of graph may be called vertex-labeled. Graphs which have labeled edges are called edge-labeled graphs.

Graphs with labels attached to edges or vertices are more generally designated as labeled. Consequently, graphs in which vertices are indistinguishable and edges are indistinguishable are called unlabeled.

Operations on Graphs: There are several operations that produce new graphs from old ones. These can be classified into the following categories (Social Network, 2011, p. 67):

- *Elementary Operations*: also called "editing operations" on graphs, which create a new graph from the original one by a local change, such as addition or deletion of a vertex or an edge, merging and splitting of vertices and so on.

- *Graph Rewrite Operations*: replacing the occurrence of some pattern graph within the host graph by an instance of the corresponding replacement graph.

- *Unary Operations*: creating a significantly new graph from the old one. Examples include: line graph, dual graph and complement graph.

- *Binary Operations*: creating a new graph from two initial graphs. Examples include: disjoint union of graphs, Cartesian product of graphs, tensor product of graphs, strong product of graphs and lexicographic product of graphs.

Graph Traversals: The way through which network analysis tools, such as Pajek, UCINET and others, analyze network data is that they apply specific algorithms, some of which are designed to find shortest path between two points, others are meant to walk the entire network to understand or sample its structure. However; all of them have the same common characteristics:

- **Depth-First Traversal:** It is an uninformed search that systematically traverses nodes until it finds its goal. This algorithm comprises descending down a child's child and then backtracks to each of its siblings. DFS can produce a spanning tree of the nodes it has visited. The edges that led to newly discovered nodes are maintained as (discovery edges) and the edges that were used for backtracking are maintained as (back edges). These two types of edges, alongside with the visited nodes, establish the spanning tree. There is also an iterative version of the standard algorithm which includes a stack to maintain visited nodes (Tsvetovat & Kouznetsov, 2011, p. 25-33).

- **Breadth-First Traversal**: The breadth-first search algorithm finds the shortest path from a single source vertex (s) to every other vertex in the same network component on both directed and undirected networks. It can be used, as well, to calculate the shortest distance between a single pair of nodes. Breadth-first search can also discover, with minor modifications, if there is more than one geodesic path between two nodes. The way breadth-first search finds the shortest is as follows (Fig. **12**): we know only that (s) has distance 0 from itself and the distances to all other vertices are unknown. Now we find all the neighbors of (s), which by definition have distance 1 from (s). Then we find all the neighbors of those vertices. Excluding those already visited, these vertices must have distance 2 and their neighbors, excluding those already visited, have distance 3 and so on (Newman, 2010, P: 231).

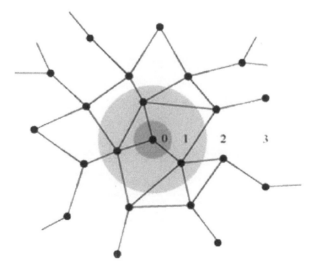

Figure 12: Breadth-first search. The search starts at a given vertex, and grows in layers or waves. (Source: Newman, 2010, p. 231).

- **Dijkstra's Algorithm:** The algorithm was published by Edsger Dijkstra in 1959 and forms the core of many so-called routing algorithms that are used in the Internet. It is considered one of the most important algorithms in modern communication networks. Dijkstra's algorithm finds the shortest path from a given node to every other node in the same network by taking the lengths of edges into account. This goes by keeping a record of the shortest path it has found so far to each vertex and updating that record whenever a shorter one is found. At the end of the algorithm, the shortest distance is found to each vertex (Newman, 2010, p. 240).

2.3.2. Trees

A tree is an undirected graph in which any two vertices are connected by one simple path. A tree G should satisfy any of the following equivalent conditions (Social Network, 2011, p. 96):

- G is connected and has no cycles.

- G has no cycles, and a simple cycle is formed if any edge is added to G.

- G is connected, and it is not connected anymore if any edge is removed from G.

- G is connected and the 3-vertex complete graph is not a minor of G.

- Any two vertices in G can be connected by a unique simple path.

Some facts about trees are as follows:

- Every tree is a bipartite graph and a median graph. Every tree with only countably many vertices is a planar graph.

- Every connected graph G admits a spanning tree, which is a tree that contains every vertex of G and whose edges are edges of G.

- Every connected graph with only countably many vertices admits a normal spanning tree.

- There exist connected graphs with uncountably many vertices which do not admit a normal spanning tree.

- Every finite tree with n vertices, with $n > 1$, has at least two terminal vertices. This minimal number of terminal vertices is characteristic of path graphs; the maximal number, $n - 1$, is attained by star graphs.

- For any three vertices in a tree, the three paths between them have exactly one vertex in common.

A *forest* is an undirected graph, all of whose connected components are trees; in other words, it consists of a disjoint union of trees.

A *polytree* or oriented tree is a directed graph with at most one undirected path between any two vertices. In other words, a polytree is a directed acyclic graph for which there are no undirected cycles either, while a *directed tree* is a directed graph which would be a tree if the directions on the edges were ignored.

A tree is called a *rooted tree* if one vertex has been designated the root, in which case the edges have a natural orientation, towards or away from the root. A rooted tree, which is a subgraph of some graph G, is a *normal tree* if the ends of every edge in G are comparable in this tree-order whenever those ends are vertices of the tree. In a context where trees are supposed to have a root, a tree without any designated root is called a *free tree*. In a rooted tree, the parent of a vertex is the vertex connected to it on the path to the root; every vertex except the root has a unique parent. A child of a vertex v is a vertex of which v is the *parent*. A *leaf* is a vertex without children.

A *labeled tree* is a tree in which each vertex is given a unique label. The vertices of a labeled tree on n vertices are typically given the labels 1, 2 ...n (Fig. **13**).

A *recursive tree* is a labeled rooted tree where the vertex labels respect the tree order (*i.e.*, if $u < v$ for two vertices u and v, then the label of u is smaller than the label of v). An *ordered tree* is a rooted tree for which an ordering is specified for the children of each vertex.

An n-ary tree is a rooted tree for which each vertex which is not a leaf has at most n children. 2-ary trees are sometimes called *binary trees*, while 3-ary trees are sometimes called *ternary trees*. A terminal vertex of a tree is a vertex of degree 1. In a rooted tree, the leaves are all terminal vertices; additionally, the root, if not a leaf itself, is a terminal vertex if it has precisely one child.

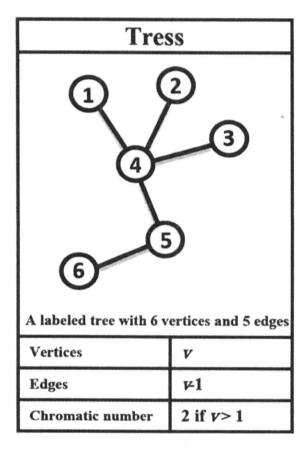

Tress	
A labeled tree with 6 vertices and 5 edges	
Vertices	V
Edges	V-1
Chromatic number	2 if $V > 1$

Figure 13: A tree example with 6 vertices and 5 edges. (Source: Social Network, 2011, p. 96).

2.3.3. Matrices

A matrix is simply an array of elements. It is an alternative way to represent and summarize network data. It contains exactly the same information as a graph.

However, it is more suitable for computation and computer analysis. Matrix operations have been widely used for definition and calculation in SNA.

Both graph and matrix operations have served as the foundations of many concepts in the analysis of social networks.

In general, a matrix is a collection of rows and columns, and the cell that emerges from the intersection of a row and a column shows the opinion of the element in the row towards the element in the column.

A matrix could be in any of the following types (Abraham *et al.*, 2010, p. 15-16):

- Column Matrix: a matrix that has vertical entries only (Fig. **14 -a**).

- Row Matrix: a matrix with only horizontal entries (Fig. **14 -b**).

- Square Matrix: a one where the number of rows and columns are equal (Fig. **14 -c**).

- Identity Matrix: a square matrix where the main diagonal has just 1s, while the rest of the elements are all 0s (Fig. **14 -d**).

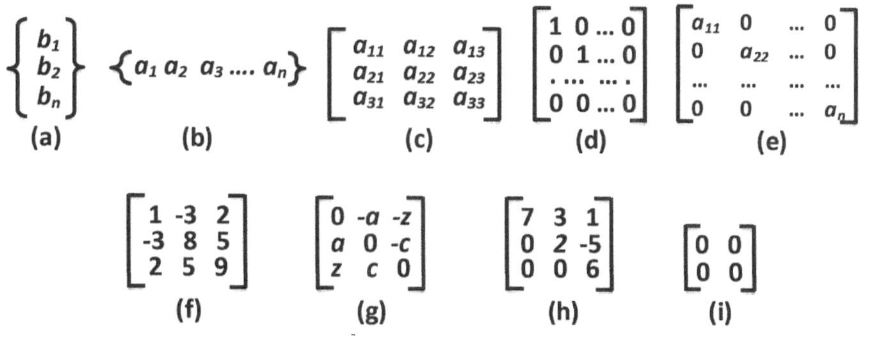

$$\begin{Bmatrix} b_1 \\ b_2 \\ b_n \end{Bmatrix} \quad \{a_1 \; a_2 \; a_3 \; .... \; a_n\} \quad \begin{bmatrix} a_{11} & a_{12} & a_{13} \\ a_{21} & a_{22} & a_{23} \\ a_{31} & a_{32} & a_{33} \end{bmatrix} \quad \begin{bmatrix} 1 & 0 & ... & 0 \\ 0 & 1 & ... & 0 \\ . & ... & ... & . \\ 0 & 0 & ... & 0 \end{bmatrix} \quad \begin{bmatrix} a_{11} & 0 & ... & 0 \\ 0 & a_{22} & ... & 0 \\ ... & ... & ... & ... \\ 0 & 0 & ... & a_n \end{bmatrix}$$

(a)   (b)   (c)   (d)   (e)

$$\begin{bmatrix} 1 & -3 & 2 \\ -3 & 8 & 5 \\ 2 & 5 & 9 \end{bmatrix} \quad \begin{bmatrix} 0 & -a & -z \\ a & 0 & -c \\ z & c & 0 \end{bmatrix} \quad \begin{bmatrix} 7 & 3 & 1 \\ 0 & 2 & -5 \\ 0 & 0 & 6 \end{bmatrix} \quad \begin{bmatrix} 0 & 0 \\ 0 & 0 \end{bmatrix}$$

(f)   (g)   (h)   (i)

Figure 14: Types of Matrices- (a) Column matrix (b) Row matrix (c) Square matrix (d) Identity matrix (e) Diagonal matrix (f) Symmetric matrix (g) Skew-symmetric matrix (h) Triangle matrix (i) Null matrix.

- Diagonal Matrix: a square matrix where all elements not on the main diagonal are 0s, while the entries on the main diagonal are not necessarily 1s (Fig. **14 -e**).

- Symmetric Matrix: a square matrix that is the same as its transpose (Fig. **14 -f**).

- Skew-Symmetric Matrix: is a square matrix in which its negative is equal to its transpose (Fig. **14 -g**).

- Triangle Matrix: a square matrix where all coefficient below the main diagonal are 0s (Fig. **14 -h**).

- Null Matrix: a matrix where all elements are zero (Fig. **14 -i**).

Types of Matrices used in Social Networks: mainly, there are three types of matrix that are used to represent social network data. These are:

Adjacency Matrix: for a directed graph, an adjacency matrix would look like this:

	A	B	C	D	E
A	0	1	0	0	0
B	1	0	0	1	0
C	0	0	0	1	1
D	1	0	1	0	0
E	1	0	1	0	0

A "1" in cell AB, for example, means that there's a relationship (edge) between nodes A and B, while "0" expresses in inexistence of such a relation. In case of a valued directed graph, the matrix would look like this:

	A	B	C	D	E
A	0	2	0	5	4
B	2	0	0	1	0

C 0 0 0 3 4

D 6 2 3 0 0

E 5 3 4 0 0

The major disadvantage of adjacency matrices is that zeros take the same amount of memory as the other cells. In fact, over 90% of cells would be zeros in a real social network. Therefore; Adjacency matrices are difficult to manipulate in practice, especially with large networks.

- Edge List Matrix:

Here, we merely list the edges of a graph *G* by specifying for each edge which vertices it is incident with. However, this representation grows linearly with the number of edges. It should also be noted that by going through this list, we also find the vertices of the associated graph, since each vertex is incident with at least one edge (Maarten, 2010, P: 33).

From	To	Value
A	B	2
A	D	5
A	E	5
B	A	2
C	E	4
D	A	5
E	C	4

- Adjacency List: In the adjacency list, searching is fast, adding and removing nodes and edges is easy—however, this structure is awkward to parse from text files or write to databases. Example:

From	Edges
A	(B 2), (D 5), (E 5)

...

Basic Matrix Operations: let's take a look at the basic matrix operations.

- *Vocabulary*: the size of a matrix is defined as the number of rows and columns in the matrix. If a matrix has the same number of rows and columns then it is square, otherwise, it is rectangular. Each entry in a matrix is called a cell. For a square matrix, the main diagonal of the matrix consists of the entries for which the index of the row is equal to the index of the column.

- *Matrix Permutation*: sometimes the pattern of ties between actors is not clear until we permute both the rows and the columns of the matrix. Matrix permutation is the rearrangement of rows and columns in a matrix, as it is sometimes useful to rearrange the rows and columns to highlight patterns in the network. Matrix permutation is important in the study of cohesive subgroups, in constructing block models, in evaluating the goodness of fit of block models. Matrix permutations are also useful if the graph is bipartite.

- *Matrix Transpose*: the transpose of a matrix is constructed by interchanging the rows and columns of the original matrix. The matrix for a digraph is not necessarily identical to its transpose, since the sociomatrix for a directional relation is not symmetric in general.

- *Matrix Addition*: the addition of a matrix of the same size is the sum of the elements in the corresponding cells of the matrices.

- *Matrix Subtraction*: it is the difference between the elements in the corresponding cells of the matrices.

- *Matrix Multiplication*: it is the product of two matrices. Matrix multiplication is very important in SNA as it can be used to study walks and reachability and is the basis for compounding relations in the analysis of relational algebras.

2.3.4. Maps

This prototype helps SN users accomplish different tasks by providing a visual model of a member's personal SN.

The task could be remembering who was in their social network, remembering connections between different people, remembering details about contacts, *etc.* This allows users to organize their SN through using a visual map of contacts and groups (Fig. **15**) (Abraham *et al.*, 2010, p. 17 and Nardi *et al.,* 2001).

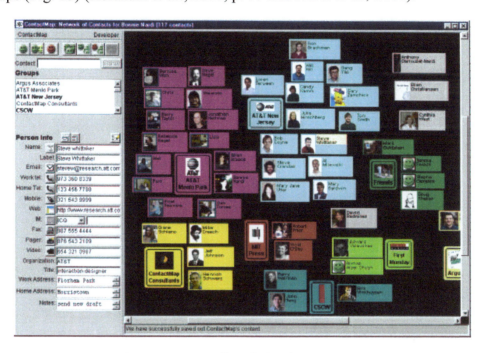

Figure 15: Map representation. (Source: Nardi *et al.*, 2001).

2.3.5. Hybrid Approach

This technique has adopted a hybrid, multidimensional visualization method that uses graphs, maps and maybe both, based on users' needs. It can provide both an egocentric and a whole view of the social network data. The method has been experimented successfully in scientific seminars.

The basic idea of this method is to simulate SN and to facilitate data management. Besides, the approach is supposed to visualize individuals and fields of interest using 3D visualization. Two dimensions of colored areas are connected to fields of interest, and the third dimension to represent the importance of each member of the SN. The importance of this type comes from its ability to show member's social significance, *i.e.* the social role of each member (Fig. **16**) (Abraham *et al.*, 2010, p. 18-19).

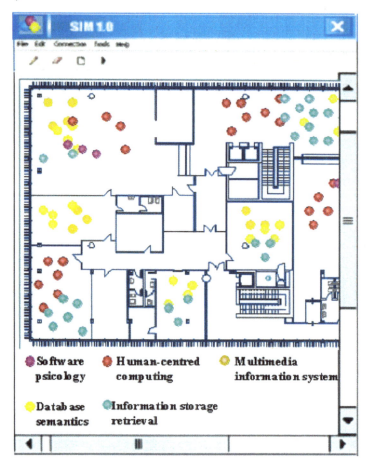

Figure 16: Hybrid network data representation (Source: Caschera *et al.*, 2008).

2.4. CONCLUSIONS

We have seen that researchers use a number of techniques for collecting data. These techniques include traditional methods such as questionnaires (the mostly used technique for data collection), people interviews, observations of actions between users and archival records. Data of online nature can be collected through using techniques such as collecting data from OSN, surveys and deploying custom applications.

When it is difficult or unworthy examining the whole collected data, researchers are forced to follow a different approach by taking a sample of the original data, and inference made about the populations of actors from the sample. Various sampling techniques have been devised such as the snow ball network sampling and the ego-centered sampling.

For network data visualization, techniques such as graphs, trees, matrices, maps and hybrid approaches have been used.

In the second part of our book and in order to apply our analysis methods, we are going to use data already made available online by GroupLens research group. The data were collected in a 4-week crawl in 2004 from the Book Crossing website, a community where users around the world share their ratings on books. The reason for conducting our analysis based on data taken from an online social network is that OSN contain large quantities of personal information. These data, in addition to providing information on users, they describe the social interactions between those users, which will be of a great importance during our study.

However, we couldn't make use of the whole chunk of the available data for a number of reasons: such as the low density of user ratings which makes predictions so noisy and the erroneous and incompleteness within demographic information. Also that data contain implicit ratings in, addition to the explicit ones, which will not be so helpful within our analysis. Therefore, we had to take a sample of the original data through a process that will be discussed broadly in chapter 4.

Although matrices have been historically widely used for network visualization, they are rarely used today due to the limited number of entries that can be used against the large size of online networks. Therefore, we are going to rely mainly on graphs to generate visualizations of networks through the use of Pajek which is a specialized tool for analyzing and visualizing large-scale networks. However, in some times, only specific parts of a network are going to be visualized so that viewers will not have problem capturing the main elements of the network.

Send Orders for Reprints to reprints@benthamscience.net

CHAPTER 3

State of the Art on SNA Applications

Abstract: Social network analysis has been used to enhance the performance or to solve problems of a wide range of applications such as semantic Web, social recommender systems, group formation *etc.* In this chapter we are going to address the main fields that SNA has contributed in their development. We will present the main contribution and summary of work for researchers in each field.

Keywords: Semantic Web, social recommender systems, group formation, software development, health, cybercrime, business, collaborative learning, animal social networks, communications. Filtering, epidemiology, distance-learning, weblog, SPARQL, FAOF.

Applications of SNA fall into two groups of research: descriptive and explanative. In descriptive applications, the focus is on structural aspects. Triadic structures, reciprocity, degree distribution and others are among the measures used here. In the other type, explanative applications, researchers are interested in explaining how attributes of nodes are dependent on their structural embedding within the network (Friemel, 2008, p.11).

Among the tasks that SNA is involved in are: identifying most important actors in SN by using centrality analysis, community detection, identifying the role associated with each member through conducting role analysis, network modeling for large-scale complex networks, how the information diffuses in a network and viral marketing (Tang & Liu, 2010, p.2). SNA can be used to identify information breakdowns, structural holes and isolated components. It can also be used to strengthen the effectiveness of existing communication channels, leverage peer support, improve innovation and learning and finally refine strategies (Serrat, 2009). We enlist below some of the most important fields of research relevant to SNA:

3.1. SEMANTIC WEB

The idea of semantic Web is to implement advanced knowledge techniques to fill the gap between machine and human. This implies providing the required

Seifedine Kadry and Mohammed Z. Al-Taie

knowledge that enables a computer to easily process and reason (Mika, 2007, p. 9).

While SNA represents social networks through the use of techniques such as degree centrality, closeness centrality, betweenness centrality, community detection, cliques and others, semantic Web uses semantic Web frameworks: It uses graph models (*e.g.* RDF), query languages (*e.g.* SPARQL) and type and definition languages (*e.g.* OWL) for online social networks. While several ontologies are used to represent social networks, the most popular one is FAOF= "Friend-Of-A-Friend" that is used to describe people, their relations and their activities.

Ereteo *et al.* (2008) introduced the concept of "Semantic Social Network Analysis" which combines features from social network analysis and semantic Web. They have designed architecture for a new tool to analyze OSNs. This tool explores RDF-based annotations describing profiles and interactions of users through social applications.

Ereteo (2011), in his PhD thesis, merged the semantic Web frameworks (which allows representing and exchanging knowledge through Web application) and SNA (that is used to characterize the structure of SN) for analyzing and structuring semantically captured social data. He goes beyond the mining of the flat link structure of social graphs by integrating a semantic processing of the network typing and the shared knowledge that emerges from online activities. His new model can bring online data to ontology-based formation, to conduct a rich semantic SNA and semantically detect communities of OSN.

3.2. SOCIAL RECOMMENDER SYSTEMS

SNA can help in making recommendations by exploring relationships between users, since customer's decision to buy a product is largely influenced by her friends, acquaintances, and others.

Recommender systems are software tools and techniques used to provide suggestions for items to be of use to users. A number of algorithms have been devised to recommend items to users such as (i) Content-Based Filtering (CBF):

the system recommends items that are similar to the ones that the user liked in the past, (ii) Collaborative Filtering (CF): the system recommends to the active user the items that other users with similar tastes liked in the past, (iii) Demographic: the system recommends items based on the demographic profile of the user, (iv) Knowledge-Based: the system recommends items based on specific domain knowledge about how certain item features meet user's needs and preferences, (v) Community-Based: This type of system recommends items based on the preferences of the users friends and (vi) Hybrid Recommender Systems: These RSs are based on the combination of the above mentioned techniques (Ricci, *et al.,* 2010, p: 1-13).

Although CF approach is the most widely used technique in recommender systems, it suffers from a number of drawbacks such as the inability to recommend new items to users and the sparse data problem which makes the prediction of accurate recommendations difficult. SNA is one tool that can remedy these drawbacks by investigating the direct and indirect transaction relationships of customers and by discovering the similarity of customers from their social communications such as transactions, purchasing behaviors and so on (Xu *et al.*, 2009).

Bohn, Feinerer, Hornik and Mair (2011) proposed an approach that aims at combing two analytic methods; the content-based filtering method and the SNA method. The reason for that combination is that the text mining technique is used to capture the text without paying attention to the social structure; a situation requires the use of SNA. With the help of using R-mailing lists, R-help and R-devel, the combination can be used to describe people's interests in order to find out whether authors with the same interests communicate or not. The results of this study showed that the relationship between sharing interests and communication exists only for very active authors, while less active authors do not answer everyone who has similar interests.

In order to enhance the performance of recommender systems, Kim, K-J. and Ahn, H. (2012) proposed a new approach that combines SNA with collaborative filtering recommender systems. One of the aims of this model is to handle one limitation of CF recommender systems which is the inability to distinguish neighbors as friends or strangers with similar taste, since qualitative and emotional information among users are not considered by standard recommender systems. This distinguishing between friends and strangers in RS is important because users prefer recommendations from friends to those from strangers. The new approach, through incorporating SNA, is able to distinguish friends and strangers and thus providing qualitative and emotional information between members of the same community. The use of SNA in this approach came by showing the social structure of users as a graph and the centrality of each user using one of the centrality measures studied before. From that graph, subgroups of users are extracted and the core of each subgroup is determined. The importance of these subgroups is that they provide important information about the influence of the subgroup on the original network as a whole and on the individual characteristics and status within the subgroup, among subgroups and the entire network.

3.3. GROUP FORMATION

The success of any project is based not only on the expertise of the people in the team, but also on how effectively they collaborate, communicate and work together. Group formation of online people with specific qualifications is becoming increasingly important these days due to the growth of online communities and social networking sites, such as Facebook and MySpace, without and explicit involvement of individuals thus making the group formation process faster and easier.

Lappas *et al.*, (2009) have considered the problem of finding a group of individuals who can function as a team to accomplish a specific task. Their basic idea is that there exists a pool of candidates, where each candidate has a set of skills. These candidates are organized in a weighted and undirected social graph. Given a task that requires a set of skills, their goal was to find a set of individuals, such that every required skill is exhibited by at least one individual. These weights can be interpreted in different ways in different application domains. For example, in a company, the weight between two employees may correlate to the length of the path from one employee to another through the organizational chart. In a scientific research community, the weight between two scientists is related to the total number of publications they have coauthored. Interpersonal relationships among individuals can also be used to calculate the weights. The authors have evaluated their group formation algorithm through using a dataset extracted from the Digital Bibliography and Library Project (DBLP) server. Their results showed that the algorithm succeeded in its work and has produced teams of experts of reasonable size in specific fields of science.

3.4. SOFTWARE DEVELOPMENT

Existing methods of social network analysis allow for locating expertise, providing better co-worker awareness, and supporting personnel development.

SNA is considered very important in software engineering when using collaborative software platforms as more and more projects have to be conducted in globally-distributed settings. These platforms bear the potential information for facilitating distributed projects through adequate information supply. For example, Kramer, Hildenbrand and Acker (2009) developed a method and a tool implementation to apply SNA techniques in distributed collaborative software development, as this provides surpassing information on expertise location, coworker activities and personnel development.

For Meneely, Williams, Snipes and Osborne (2008), they applied SNA to code churn information, as an additional means to predict software failures. Code churn is a software development artifact, common to most large projects, and is used to predict failures at the file level. They conducted their research based on a case study from a large Nortel networking product, comprising more than 11000 files and three million lines of code. Their goal was to examine human factor in failure predicting.

3.5. HEALTH

Network analysis, more and more, is becoming well-known in infectious disease epidemiology, such as HIV and Sexually Transmitted Diseases (STD). Also, a strong trend is emerging towards using inter-organizational network analysis to detect patterns of health care delivery such as service integration and collaboration (Hawe, Webster & Shiell, 2004).

The contribution of SNA to health falls in five categories (Valente, 2010, p. 36):

- The influence of social support on mortality and morbidity.

- The influence of network theory and modeling on AIDS/STDs and family planning research.

- The effect of SNA on community health projects to enhance message dissemination and program implementation.

- A number of researches related to inter-organizational collaboration, cooperation and exchange studies have been done for the sake of better understanding to health service provisioning.

- The help of SNA to understand and enhance the performance of health care providers.

Perisse and Nery (2007) conducted a study to know the relationship between SNA and the epidemiology and prevention of STD. They argue that SNA will be of a great utility in the study of STD.

Gardy *et al.* (2011) found that traditional contact tracing (the technique they used at the beginning of their search to discover the reason behind the spread of *tuberculosis* in a medium-size community in British Colombia) did not identify the source of the disease. By using whole-Genome sequencing and SNA, they discovered that the cause was related to socio-environmental factor.

3.6. CYBERCRIME

Yang and Ng (2007) presented a framework to analyze and visualize weblog social networks. A weblog is a website where the contents are formulated in a diary style and maintained by the blogger. This environment constitutes a suitable operation platform for organizing crimes. With the ability to analyze and visualize weblog social networks in crime-related matters, intelligence agencies will have additional techniques to secure the society.

To investigate hacker community, Lu, Polgar, Luo and Cao (2010) examined the social structure of an unknown hacker community called 'Shadowcrew'. In their investigation, they used text mining and network analysis to discover the relationships among hackers. Based on the analysis conducted, they found that that community exhibits features of deviant team organization structure and the decentralized composition of that community.

3.7. BUSINESS

SNA applies to a wide range of business fields, including human resources, knowledge management and collaboration, team building, sales and marketing and strategy. We will restrict ourselves here to few examples only:

Hatala (2006), in his study, looked at SNA as a tool which can enhance the empirical quality of Human Resource Development (HRD) theory in areas such as organizational development, organizational learning, *etc.* He argues that SNA will add much to the HRD fields by measuring the relations between individuals, and the effect those relations have on human capital output. Also, it will help further by developing the field of HRD through enabling researchers to analyze the interaction between individuals and the surrounding.

Doshi, Krauss, Nann and Gloor (2009) studied influence of SNA and sentiment analysis in predicting business trends. They focused on predicting the successes of new movies, in the box office, for the first four weeks. They were trying to predict prices on the Hollywood stock exchange, and the ratio of gross income to the budget of the production. They depended on data posts from the Internet Movie Database (IMDb) forums to get sentiment metrics for positivity and negativity based on forum discussions.

Through Twitter, Zhang, Fuehres and Gloor (2010) tried to predict stock market indicators such as Dow Jones, S&P500 and NASDAQ. They took about one hundredth of the total Twitter data that covered six months of activity. Through analyzing the relationship between data and stock market indicators, they found that emotional tweets displayed negative correlation to NASDAQ and S&P500, but gave positive correlation to VIX. Their results show that Twitter analysis can be a tool to predict stock market of the next day.

Coscia, Giannotti and Pensa (2009) presented a new methodology for mining knowledge based on digital bibliography as a case study, as these bibliographies have been widely used in many studies focusing specifically on knowledge extraction from databases. For the task of knowledge mining, they have applied SNA. They also applied some data mining techniques in order to evolve a complete methodology.

Also, Kakimoto, Kamei, Ohira and Matsumoto (2006) studied the influence of SNA on knowledge collaboration in OSS communities. After using communication tools (such as mailing lists, discussion forums, *etc.*) they applied SNA to data accumulated in these communication tools. As a case study, they took Forge.net website and started investigating the quality of communications for knowledge collaboration. They found that communications among community members with various roles were actively encouraged when OSS was released, as knowledge collaboration was doing well.

3.8. COLLABORATIVE LEARNING

Reffay and Chanier (2003) showed that concepts of SNA, adapted to the collaborative distant-learning, can assist measuring the cohesion of small groups. Their data were taken from distance-learning experiment of ten weeks. They used different ways to measure cohesion for the sake of highlighting active subgroups, isolated people and roles of members. This thing has to show global attributes at the group level and individual level, and will help the tutor in following the collaboration in the group.

Penuel *et al.*, (2006) investigated the potential use of SNA to evaluate the programs which seek to enhance school performance through encouraging greater collaboration among teachers. By gathering data about teacher collaboration with schools, they could map the distribution of expertise and resources needed to achieve reforms. These maps would be of a great importance to headmasters.

3.9. ANIMAL SOCIAL NETWORKS

The analysis of animal social structures can intensify our understanding towards the social dynamics of animal populations and can suggest new management methods. However, in spite of the similarities that exist between human and animal social networks, it is harder to study the social networks of animals since techniques such as interviews and questionnaires are not used and network data gathering can only be implemented through direct observation of interactions between individuals.

Wey, T. *et al.,* (2007) believe that SNA methods can help improve our realization of the complex relationships, the social structure of animal gatherings and the direct and indirect interactions between group members.

Lusseau, D. and Newman, M. (2004) used techniques taken from social network analysis to analyze the social network of a community of dolphins living in New Zealand. They have used the "betweenness" measure to identify the possible communities and sub-communities within the dolphin population. In addition, they identified the existence of centralized "brokers" in this community, located between communities. Those brokers may play a crucial role in maintaining the cohesiveness of the dolphin community. The betweenness centrality measure was again used in this identification.

In a different study, Berger-Wolf, T. *et al.,* (2010) used the dynamic social network analysis- the use of temporal information to identify communities with high intra-community interactions in order to investigate their development, persistence and decline of their life time- to study the differences between two animal species: the Grevy's zebra found in eastern Africa and the Onagers, wild assess widespread from the Middle East to India.

Also, Barale, C. (2010) used techniques of SNA, such as centrality measures, to identify the influential members in a sheep network of 19 individuals in Kenya. The importance of such identification is that those individuals may lead group movements and influence group consolidation when subgroups disperse.

3.10. COMMUNICATIONS

Tomar *et al.* (2010), in their study, have analyzed various structural properties of Short Message Service (SMS) graphs. The graphs were induced by people exchanging SMSs, while the entries of these graphs were obtained from one service provider. The authors believe that the use of SNA can provide a thorough analysis of the SMS behavior of users and thus increase both utilization of network resources and revenue of the operator. Measures, such as the in-degree distribution, out-degree distribution, connected components and cliques were used. In those weighted graphs, the customers are represented by vertices and the SMS transactions are represented by edges and weights (Fig. **17**). The analysis results show that the use of in-degree distribution and out-degree distribution helped in identifying spammers. Also, it was found that 70% of the components are of size two (isolated pairs).

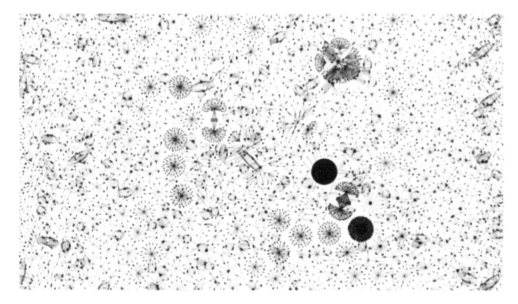

Figure 17: Visualization of social interaction in SMS transactions. (Source: Tomar *et al.*, 2010).

In a different study, Papadimitriou *et al.* (2010) have reviewed the possible implications behind the use of SNA on wireless sensor networks in terms of theory, algorithms and applications. Sensor networks consists of sensor nodes which are spatially distributed autonomous micro devices that can be programmed to monitor a variety of chemical, physical and environmental phenomena. Today, there are some industrial areas where these sensors had the biggest impact. For example, they are being used in habitat monitoring, traffic monitoring and health care. Latest statistics refer that, due to traffic accidents, more than one million people, worldwide, are killed while more than fifty million people are injured every year. Here, Sensor technology has been applied to help providing the required level of safety. Since "betweenness" measure assesses the number of shortest paths passing through a given node or edge, it was borrowed by sensor networks such that large values of betweenness for a sensor may point out that this sensor can reach other sensors on relatively short paths. However, this requires the detailed knowledge of the connectivity of its one-hop neighbors. The importance of the betweenness centrality measure, here, is to know the distribution of the position of vehicles, the highest-quality nodes (vehicles), how to spread the message with the minimal number of rebroadcasts so as to reduce collisions and latency, the distribution of synapses per node and for the identification of bridge nodes which are in charged with the delivery/ferrying of the message when the network is disconnected (Fig. **18**).

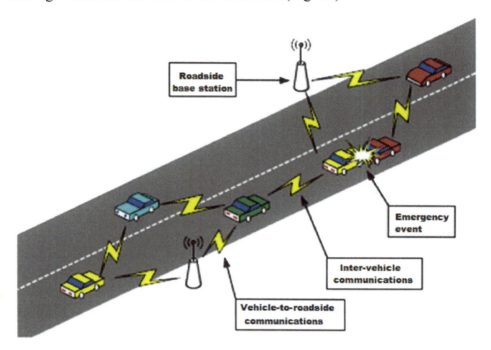

Figure 18: Intervehicle communications. (Source: Papadimitriou *et al.*, 2010).

Holzer, Malin and Sweeney (2005) conducted a new research to investigate the problem of correctly relating aliases that affiliate to the same entity by using SNA rather than traditional natural language processing and structured data. They took a dataset consisting of over 14000 university email addresses for which ground truth relations are known. The analysis of email addresses has shown that most aliases tend to happen closely to each other, half of email aliases are within a geodesic distance of two from each other, and that 20% of aliases are directly connected.

CHAPTER 4

Research Methods and Procedures

Abstract: In this chapter, we are going to apply specific techniques of SNA to analyze the BX-dataset (The data that was crawled from the Book Crossing website in 2004) (Fig. **19**) and dig out some results such as most positively-rated books (most popular books) and most active users and so on. Then, we are going to conduct the analysis of the user-user network, a sub-network that generates from partitioning the user-preference network. The analysis will take us to apply techniques related to centrality degrees to discover most important figures in that sub-network, in addition to the ego-network analysis and the m-slice analysis.

Keywords: Affiliation networks, network analysis, centrality measures, ego network, brokerage roles, m-slice analysis, Centrality measures, Network visualization, network partitioning, user-preference, nodes, degree, Statistical analysis, Mother-network, Data pre-processing, Bookcrossing.

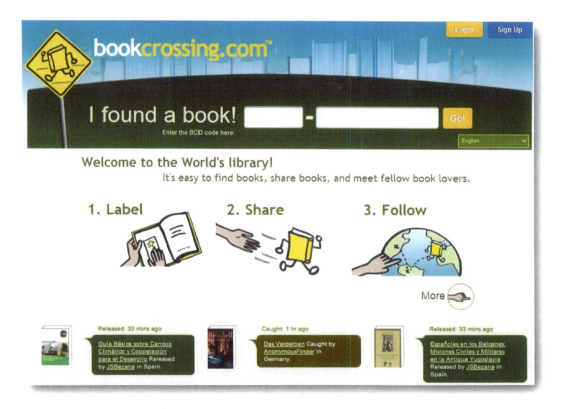

Figure 19: Home page of Bookcrossing.com.

Seifedine Kadry and Mohammed Z. Al-Taie

4.1. POPULATION AND NETWORK BOUNDARY

Network analysis investigates the relationships within a whole bounded population or sub-population rather than a sample of the population. Thus, network boundaries create the population of actors. For the population in this book, the network boundary is restricted only to users who at least rated one book.

4.2. NETWORK CONSTRUCTION

Within the population of actors, users will represent network actors, and a network tie exists between a user and a book if he/she rates a book on a scale from 1-10. The demographic information for each user (such as age and location) enables for more discrete data analysis, and can be considered whenever necessary.

4.3. DATA DESCRIPTION

The performance of SNA algorithms has been experimented on several datasets. In general, datasets are either artificially generated or emerge from real networks. Artificial datasets are automatically created and are used to qualify and compare different community detection algorithms, while real datasets are mainly used for evaluating the effectiveness of an algorithm to analyze SN.

The dataset that we use in this book (available for free download from the Internet) has two file types: '.sql' and '.csv'. The second file type is considered due to the ease of use and manipulation. With the powerful functions in Excel for data management, it can be used to store and organize relational data and to put these data in files readable by other specialized packages.

Three files are extracted (in the case of.csv file): BX-Books, BX-Users and BX-Book-Ratings. The BX-Books file contains information about the books available in the website database: ISBN, Book-Title, Book Author, Year of Publication, Publisher and image-URL in three sizes (large, medium and small).

The BX-Users file contains demographic information about registered users, namely location and age. The BX-Book-Ratings file contains the relational data that connect between users and rated items, in addition to the weight of relationships (expressed as a numerical value on a scale from 0 to 10).

The BX dataset was collected in a 4-week crawl (August/September 2004) by Ziegler, McNee, Konstan and Lausen (2005) from the Book Crossing, a community where users around the world exchange information about books. This dataset was made available by GroupLens research group. The dataset contains 1,149,780 implicit and explicit ratings on a scale from 0 to 10. Implicit ratings are expressed by 0 on the scale and constitute 716,109 ratings. The remaining 433,681 ratings are regarded as explicit ratings across 1 to 10 on the scale. The total number of users is 278,858 and the number of the books is 271,379 (H. Sun, Peng, Chen, Liu & Y. Sun, 2011).

Huang and Jebara (2010) argue that BX dataset also contains many more implicit preferences, like when users buy books they do not explicitly rate them, which indicates positive opinions of those books.

One of the benefits that BX dataset has, over the other public datasets such as MySpace dataset, is that it is less noisy, due to the fact that the users of BX community do not supply item names through free text, a situation if occurs requires correctly matching identical items (Shani, Chickering & Meek, 2008).

However; BX dataset suffers, like any other public dataset, from a number of drawbacks such as low density of user ratings, a problem which makes predictions so noisy in this context. This issue forced other researchers to take only a subset of the BX dataset (Cortes, Mohri & Rastogi, 2007). In addition, the demographic information contains what it looks erroneous and incomplete data. Also, if the dataset were to have more demographic information (such as gender or occupation) we would have had more deep understanding of user preference shapes.

Based on content, Zhang, Cao and Yeung (2010) discretized the BX-dataset into five general domains (Table 1):

Table 1: BX-Dataset taxonomy (based on book content) (Source: Zhang *et al.*, 2010)

Domain #1	Domain #2	Domain #3	Domain #4	Domain #5
Mystery and Thrillers	Science Fiction and Fantasy	Science	Business and Investing	Religion and Spirituality

4.4. DATA PRE-PROCESSING

Removing implicit ratings, namely those with values equal to 0 on the scale, is necessary since implicit ratings are written reviews rather than numerical values. This act was followed by most of the researchers whose studies where surveyed. So, from the original dataset which comprised 1,149,780 ratings, we are left only with 433,659 ratings (on a scale from 1 to 10).

The procedure could have been done using Pajek based on tie weights. However; since it is a very huge dataset, we are neither able to import the whole data set one time to Pajek, nor are able to split up the data into small units. Usually, one sheet of MS Excel file has the limit of 1,048,576 rows and 16,384 columns. Therefore; this procedure can be done using MS Access 2010. Moving from MS Access towards MS Excel 2010, we transform the (.xls) file into (.txt) file for a later conversion to Pajek-compatible file. Using the freely available software (txt2pajek), we convert the (.txt) file into (.net) file, which is now executable on Pajek.

4.5. TWO-MODE NETWORK ANALYSIS

A 2-mode network (also called Affiliation, Bimodal and Bipartite networks) has two types of nodes, and the link determines the relationships between one set of nodes and the other set. A Two-mode network matrix representation is given in Table **2**.

Table 2: Two-mode network matrix representation

	Event 1	Event 2	Event 3
Actor 1	0	0	0
Actor 2	1	1	1

Examples of 2-mode networks include corporate board management, attendance at events, membership in clubs, participation in online groups, membership in production teams and even course-taking patterns of high school students.

Small scale 2-mode networks can be formed as a 2-mode rectangular matrix, such that rows and columns refer to two different sets of entities.

4.6. MOTHER-NETWORK

The first network that we are going to analyze is the mother network, namely the network that contains all nodes and arcs. It covers the entire scale of ratings, *i.e.* from 1 to 10 (of course after omitting implicit ratings).

Tie weights are going to be temporarily ignored at this stage and the network has no isolated nodes, since only users who had explicitly rated at least one book are considered.

Visualization of a network with more than few hundreds of nodes becomes less helpful. Also it becomes difficult for the eye to notice line incidence with vertices.

Analyzing this network will help us answering the question: which users have made the highest number of ratings (most active users)? We can also answer the question: which books obtained the highest number of ratings (No matter whether they were negative or positive)?

Statistical Analysis: Let's take a look at Table **3** to see some of the overall statistics of the mother network, evaluated using Pajek.

Table 3: Some overall statistics of the mother-network

Metric	Value
Graph Type	Directed
Dimension	263631
Number of Arcs	433660
Network Density	0.00000624
Number of Loops	0
Number of Multiple Lines	0

Table 3: *contd...*

Average Degree	3.28990142
Connected Components	14684
Single-Vertex Connected Component	0
Maximum Vertices in a Connected Component	229036 (86.877%)

It is a directed two-mode network with density equals 0.00000624, which is very low. The number of nodes (dimension) is 263631 and the number of ties is 433660 (the more number of nodes in a network, the less the network density). The network has neither loops nor multiple lines and the average degree is 3.28990142. The number of connected components is 14684, which is very high (due to the high dispersion in users' choices) and the largest component consists of 229036 nodes. The network has no isolated vertices. Based on the total number of outgoing ties, we can use the out-degree measure, which is located in the "Net /Partitions/degree/output" drop-box within Pajek, to determine the most active users in the network.

In this network, we find that there is a large component (also sometimes called giant component) that fills most of the network—constituting more than 86% of the whole network—while the rest of the network is divided into a large number of small components disconnected from the rest. This behavior of network structure, although can be found in directed networks, is typically found in undirected networks.

In many applications of networks it is crucial that there be a component that fills most of the network, such as in the Internet where it is important that there be a path through the network from most computers to most others. Without it, the network wouldn't be able to perform its job of providing computer-to-computer communications for its users (Newman, 2010, p. 294)

The highest out-degree, lowest out-degree and network output degree centralization values for the mother-network are shown in Table **4**:

Table 4: Highest out-degree, lowest out-degree and out-degree centralization values in the mother-network

Metric	Value	Frequency
Highest out degree value	8522	1
Lowest out degree value	1	45375
Network output degree Centralization	0.03231949	-

We can see that only one node has obtained the highest number of outgoing ties "8522" (representing the most active user) from among 263631 nodes, and that 45375 other nodes (approximately 1/6 of the network nodes) supplied only 1 vote (expressing the least active users). The analysis also gives us 185833 nodes with zero out-degree (not shown in the table above). This is because Pajek analyzed both types of nodes, namely users and books, and that the nodes with out-degrees equal to 0 represent books (destination of relationships).

We can also calculate the normalized values for the above results through dividing the absolute degree centrality of a node (indicated as C_{AD_i}) by the maximum possible in-degrees (n-1 nodes), and express the result as either a proportion or percentage:

$$C_{ND_i} = C_{AD_i} / (n-1)$$

The normalized in-degree centrality takes continuous values from 0 (which indicates no in-degree value) to 1 (which indicates maximum in-degree value).

The ten highest out-degree values along with their normalized values in the mother- network were as in Table **5**:

Table 5: Top ten out-degree values of the mother network

Rank	Out-Degree	Normalized Out-Degree	User ID	Age	Country
1.	8522	0.0323	11676	Null	N/A
2.	5802	0.0220	98391	52	USA
3.	1969	0.0075	153662	44	USA
4.	1906	0.0072	189835	Null	USA
5.	1395	0.0053	23902	Null	United Kingdom
6.	1036	0.0039	76499	Null	USA

Table 5: *contd…*

7.	1035	0.0039		171118	47	Canada
8.	1023	0.0039		235105	46	USA
9.	968	0.0037		16795	47	USA
10.	948	0.0036		248718	43	USA

Some users have higher out-degree values than others since they have provided a higher number of book ratings; in other word they are more active than their associates. We can see that 70-80% of the people whose outgoing links were probed were from USA, and that the average user age is between 40s and 50s, which gives an indication that older people are more interested in book reading compared to young people. Also, it looks that people from USA do more social activities than people from other countries (The same point was pointed out by Lucas, Segrera and Moreno (2008)).

In addition to the out-degree measure, we can also evaluate the in-degree measure which can be found in the "Net/Partitions/degree/input" drop-box within Pajek. It calculates the number of incoming arcs for each vertex so; it is a measure for determining the vertices that attracted much of users' interest.

The highest input degree, lowest input degree and input degree centralization values for the mother-network are given in Table **6**:

Table 6: Highest input degree, lowest input degree and in-degree centralization values of the mother-network

Metric	Value	Frequency
Highest input degree value	707	1
Lowest input degree value	1	129480
Network Input Degree Centralization	0.00267556	-

We can see that only one node has acquired the highest number of incoming arcs (in-degree) from among 263631 nodes, and that 129480 other nodes acquired only 1 incoming arc. We can see that the nodes, which gained only 1 vote from users for each, represent about half the mother-network.

The analysis also gives us 77798 nodes with zero incoming ties (not shown in the table above). This is because the analysis comprised both types of nodes, namely users and books, and that nodes with in-degrees equal to 0 represent users (source of relationships) so; they do not get any incoming tie.

The ten books that obtained the highest number of ratings (over the entire rating scale) are as in Table **7**:

Table 7: Top ten in-degree values of the mother-network

Rank	In-Degree	Normalized in-Degree	ISBN	Book Title
1.	707	0.0027	0316666343	The Lovely Bones: A Novel
2.	581	0.0022	0971880107	Wild Animus
3.	487	0.0018	0385504209	The Da Vinci Code
4.	383	0.0015	0312195516	The Red Tent (Bestselling Backlist)
5.	333	0.0013	0679781587	Memoirs of a Geisha: A Novel*
6.	320	0.0012	0060928336	Divine Secrets of the Ya-Ya Sisterhood: A Novel
7.	315	0.0012	059035342x	Harry Potter and the Sorcerer's Stone (Harry Potter (Paperback))
8.	307	0.0012	0142001740	The Secret Life of Bees
9.	295	0.0011	0446672211	Where the Heart Is (Oprah's Book Club (Paperback))
10.	282	0.0011	044023722x	A Painted House

The novel 'The lovely bones' has occupied position #1. This is due to the fact that it gained the largest portion of users' evaluation and attention. The normalized values come from dividing the incoming ties of a specific vertex by the possible number of incoming ties (which equals the number of vertices in the network -1). For example, 707/263630 gives us approximately 0.0027 and so on. For the book in position #5, we could not find any corresponding information in the dataset. So, we took help from Amazon.com to get the book title and other information. This is an example of the bugs existing in this dataset.

4.7. USER-PREFERENCE NETWORK

Based on tie values, it is possible to extract this network. It will comprise ratings of users who have rated items with 6 to 10 on the rating scale.

The basic idea behind the formation of this network is that our interest is to know whether a user recommends reading/buying a book or not, which means constructing a network of 'likes' and 'dislikes' (Lowd & Davis, 2010; Weng, Zhang, Zhou, Yang, Tian & Zhong, 2009). For an ordinary reader, it doesn't make any difference if the book is good, very good or excellent as long as it is OK. However, if the book is bad, very bad or absolutely bad the consumer wouldn't make a risk to buy this book (or wasting time reading it) as long as it is not OK.

However; for a reason not revealed, Lucas *et al.* (2008) considered only ratings with 7 or more on the rating scale as the positive ones.

Tie weights were ignored in this network (after determining the population) and the network has no isolated nodes, since only those users who had rated books within 6 to 10 on the scale were considered.

Analyzing the network will help us answering the question: which books were most positively-rated (or in other words: most popular books)?

Statistical Analysis: Let's have a look at some overall statistics of the user-preference network (Table **8**):

Table 8: Overall statistics of the user-preference network

Metric	Value
Graph Type	Directed
Dimension	228970
Number of Arcs	363258
Network Density	0.00000693
Number of Loops	0
Number of Multiple Lines	0
Average Degree	3.17297463
Connected Components	13979
Single-Vertex Connected Component	0
Maximum Vertices in a Connected Component	196180 (85.679%)

It is a two-mode network consisting of 228970 nodes and 363258 arcs with no edges, since it is a relationship between a user and the book that he/she evaluates.

So, there is no meaning to consider edges. Even though the network density is low (0.00000693), it is still higher than the mother network. This is because the current network has a less number of nodes, since the largest the number of nodes is, the least the density. The largest component in this network occupies about 85.679% of the total size of the network. The highest and lowest in-degree values and the network in-degree centralization are as in Table **9**:

Table 9: Highest, lowest and in-degree centralization values of the user-preference network

Metric	Value	Frequency
Highest input degree value	663	1
Lowest input degree value	1	112010
Network Input Degree Centralization	0.00288867	

We can see that nearly half of the user-preference network nodes (*i.e.* 112010 nodes) obtained only 1 vote, and that only one book obtained the highest number of votes, namely 663. We can also determine the ten books with the highest in-degree values (representing most popular books) as shown in Table **10**:

Table 10: Top 10 in-degree values of the user-preference network

Rank	In-Degree	Normalized in-Degree	ISBN	Book Title
1.	663	0.0029	0316666343	The Lovely Bones: A Novel
2.	452	0.0020	0385504209	The Da Vinci Code
3.	344	0.0015	0312195516	The Red Tent (Bestselling Backlist)
4.	307	0.0013	0679781587	Memoirs of a Geisha: A Novel
5.	305	0.0013	059035342x	Harry Potter and the Sorcerer's Stone (Harry Potter (Paperback))
6.	292	0.0013	0142001740	The Secret Life of Bees
7.	285	0.0012	0060928336	Divine Secrets of the Ya-Ya Sisterhood: A Novel
8.	274	0.0012	0446672211	Where the Heart Is (Oprah's Book Club (Paperback))
9.	260	0.0011	0452282152	Girl with a Pearl Earring
10.	250	0.0011	0671027360	Angels & Demons

The table above lists the ten most popular books. The more in-degree value is, the more prestigious the book is. With this said, we can say that the most preferred (popular) book (at the time when the data was crawled) was "The Lovely Bones: A novel".

4.8. USER NON-PREFERENCE NETWORK

The third network that we want to analyze is the user non-preference network, which was extracted using the same method used with the two previous networks (meaning based on tie values). It comprises the users who have rated books with 1 to 5 on the rating scale. Tie values were ignored after determining the network population. Analyzing the network will help us answering the question: which books are most negatively-rated (most unpopular books)?

Statistical Analysis: let's take a look at Table **11**.

Table 11: Overall statistics of the user non-preference network

Metric	Value
Graph Type	Directed
Dimension	73716
Number of Arcs	70403
Network Density	0.00001296
Number of Loops	0
Number of Multiple Lines	0
Average Degree	1.91011449
Connected Components	10865
Single-Vertex Connected Component	0
Maximum Vertices in a Connected Component	45008 (61.056%)

As shown above, it is a two-mode network consisting of 73716 nodes and 70703 arcs with no edges or loops. Network Density equals to 0.00001296 which is very low (however, it is still higher than the two previous networks since this network has only 73716 nodes). We notice that the number of nodes here exceeds the number of arcs, which indicates users' less care to evaluate uninteresting books. The number of connected components and the average degree are less than what they are in the previous networks. It has a less average degree since the number of arcs here is less than the number of nodes. The highest and lowest in-degree values and the network in-degree centralization are as in Table **12**:

Table 12: Highest and lowest in-degree values of the user non-preference network

Metric	Value	Frequency
Highest in-degree value	389	1
Lowest in-degree value	1	41447
Network in-degree Centralization	0.00526420	

More than half of the network nodes (books) obtained only 1 vote for each, while the highest in-degree value in the user-non preference network is 389, which means that the corresponding book was rated by users as the most unpopular book.

By implementing the in-degree measure, we get the following ten results (Table **13**):

Table 13: Top in-degree values of the user non-preference network

Rank	In-Degree	Normalized In-Degree	ISBN	Book Title
1.	389	0.0053	0971880107	Wild Animus
2.	51	0.0007	044023722x	A Painted House
3.	44	0.0006	0316666343	The Lovely Bones: A Novel
4.	41	0.0006	0316601950	The Pilot's Wife : A Novel
5.	41	0.0006	0316769487	The Catcher in the Rye
6.	39	0.0005	0312195516	The Red Tent (Bestselling Backlist)
7.	39	0.0005	0446605239	The Notebook
8.	38	0.0005	0425182908	Isle of Dogs
9.	36	0.0005	0140293248	The Girls' Guide to Hunting and Fishing
10.	35	0.0005	0375727345	House of Sand and Fog

We notice that two of the books in the table above (ranks 3, 6) also appear in the user-preference network. This may reflect the fact that users' choices covered a wide range of ratings over a scale (from 1 to 10), and that people opinion towards these books largely scattered between "good" and "bad".

4.9. AFFILIATION NETWORK ANALYSIS

The term Affiliation (a synonym of 2-mode) refers to membership or participation data such as when we have data on which actors have participated in which events.

People ideas, attitudes and social connections are marked by their memberships within groups, a phenomenon defined by sociologists as 'Duality'. Also, groups are marked by the attitudes of the members, and members can exist in more than one group, which is called co-membership; a situation expressing a stronger associations between people and perhaps hints at one common identity.

Usually, an affiliation graph can be represented as a bipartite graph (V1, V2, E), where V1 and V2 are two different sets of nodes, while E is an affiliation relation between the elements of V1 and V2 (Borgatti & Halgin, 2011).

We can say that co-membership in groups or an event is an indicator of a social tie. Also, we can say that co-participation provides the opportunities for social ties to develop, which in turn gives the chance for things like innovation, information or news to flow. Affiliation data comprises binary ties (0 or 1) connecting between members of the two sets of items. So, these binary relationships are limited to partial relations such as "is a member of" or "participant in".

In Fig. **20** below, persons A and B are members of the same club. We can infer that they may know each other and that the triad is really closed. The more the links they have in common, the stronger the connection is (Tsvetovat & Kouznetsov, 2011, p. 93-97).

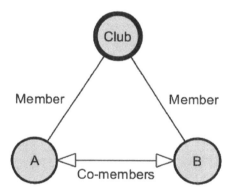

Figure 20: Affiliation network simplified.

The idea behind inducing co-affiliation network from affiliation network (which means converting a 2-mode network to two 1-mode networks) is that co-affiliation network prepares the ground for the development of social relationships between the actors of one set. For example, the more the number of times people come at the same event, the more likely those people are going to interact and develop some kind of relationship. It has been reported that persons whose activities are focused around the same point, frequently become connected over time.

Another reason for having co-affiliation networks is that affiliation data can be a consequence of having a tie, such as when a married couple attend (together) a great number of events and join the same social clubs (Borgatti & Halgin, 2011).

In 2-mode networks, there is an opportunity for people to interact, communicate and like each other. Moreover, joint membership in an organization often includes similarities in other social fields. For example, if people have chosen to become members in a chess club, they may well have similar professions, interests and even social status. It is a matter of the number of shared intensity which induces the degree of similarity of people (De Nooy *et al.*, 2005, p. 102).

Co-affiliations are analyzed to identify chances of interactions (such as flow of information) or unseen relationships between people (such as sociometric preferences). So, in order to analyze the BX-Dataset (which is basically a 2-mode network), we need (before we can use the 1-mode analysis techniques) to apply one of the two following approaches: the direct method, which includes analyzing both node-sets simultaneously, which requires the use of some special metrics and algorithms that are designed specifically for that purpose. The other approach is to use the conversion method (the one that is chosen here) which includes analyzing co-affiliations among elements of one-mode set based on their profiles over the other set (Borgatti & Halgin, 2011).

4.10. AFFILIATION NETWORK PARTITIONING

We will extract two 1-mode sub-networks from a 2-mode network: the first one is the network of interlocking events (if two books share the same event *i.e.* being read by the same two or more readers) and a network of actors (if two users or more like the same books). The *Rate of Participation* of an actor is the number of shared events, and the *Size of an Event* for a book is the number of multiple readers.

Intuitively, the density of a 1-mode network is larger than a 2-mode network since in a 1-mode network, nodes can be correlated with any other node in the network, not only with nodes of the same set (the case of a 2-mode network).

We can easily transform the network of BX-dataset into two 1-mode sub-networks using the above direct method: the first sub-network represents the user-user relationships, while the second sub-network represents item-item relationships, by applying (Net/Transform/2-mode to 1-mode/rows or columns) drop-box within Pajek, where the option "rows" gives us the item-item network and the option "columns" gives the reader-to-reader network. Pajek can efficiently do that by splitting up the list of vertices within Pajek file into two parts, each for one sub-network (De Nooy *et al.*, 2005, p. 104-106).

In Fig. **21**, user A and user C have positively rated one book so; they are likely to develop a social relationship between them. This relation will have a weight equals to 1. The same thing is true for C&D, B&D and A&B. Tie weights can increase based on the number of affiliations (in our case: books) in common.

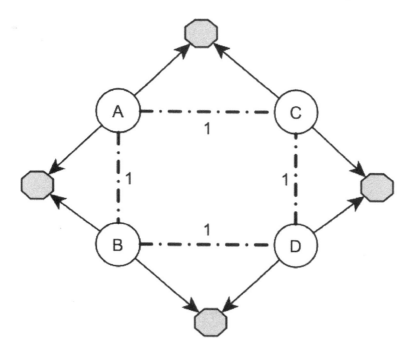

Figure 21: Affiliation network partitioning simplified.

Different from a 2-mode network, a 1-mode network refers to one set of nodes and each vertex can be related to other vertices in the same network (De Nooy *et al.*, 2005, p. 103).

A Small scale 1-mode network can be represented by a square 1-mode matrix (Table **14**), where rows and columns refer to the same set of vertices.

Table 14: One-mode network matrix representation

	Actor 1	Actor 2	Actor 3
Actor 1	0	1	0
Actor 2	1	0	1
Actor 3	1	1	0

4.11. USER-USER NETWORK

For the sake of affiliation network analysis, we will make use of the user-preference network with one difference; we will not exclude tie values from our calculations this time. This new network will help us probing the potential social relations among users.

We restrict ourselves here to extract the user-user network from the user-preference network (not the mother network), because what makes people develop friendships relies mainly on the things they share and the things they like.

Network Visualization: It is not easy (or even so helpful) to visualize a large network, especially with the many details. So, here, we eliminate vertex labels and edges between vertices. Nodes in the middle area are core nodes, while nodes around the core are periphery nodes. Fig. **22** shows a 2D representation of the user-user network. Nodes are placed according to the spring layout given by the Fruchterman- Reingold method (after its two authors, namely Thomas Fruchterman and Edward Reingold). The algorithm is a modification of the earlier spring-embedder model presented by Eades in 1984. The basic idea of this method of drawing is that vertices that are connected by an edge must be drawn near each other and that vertices should not be drawn too close to each other. How close vertices must be drawn relies on the number of vertices and the amount of space available. The idea of the displacement of a vertex is that it is limited to a maximum value, and this maximum value reduces over time. So, the final layout becomes better and the size of drawing adjustments becomes finer and finer. The two authors were inspired (while working on the new design) by some natural systems, such as macro-cosmic gravity and springs (Fruchterman & Reingold, 1991).

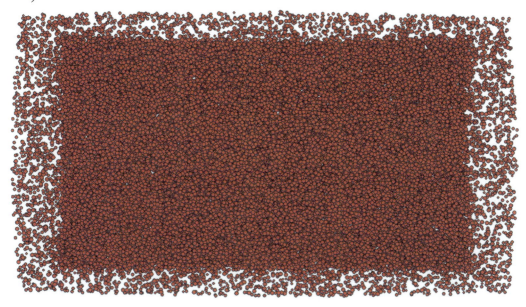

Figure 22: A 2-D representation of the user-user network. The network was energized using Fruchterman- Reingold algorithm. Edges and vertex labels have been eliminated.

Statistical Analysis: A short summary of metrics are given in Table **15**.

Table 15: Overall statistics of the user-user network

Metric	Value
Graph Type	Undirected
Dimension	69768
Number of Edges	3176585
Network Density	0.00130522
Number of Loops	0
Number of Multiple Lines	0
Connected Components	883
Single-Vertex Connected Component	13096

Table 15: *contd...*

Maximum Vertices in a Connected Component	54701(78.404%)
Maximum Geodesic Distance (Diameter)	10
Average Geodesic Distance (Among Reachable Pairs)	2.80782
Average Degree	91.06137484
Number of Unreachable Pairs	1875356164

It is a one-mode undirected sub-network consisting of 69768 vertices and 3176585 weighted edges. Network density equals to 0.001305 which is higher than the earlier networks. This is because a 1-mode network has higher density than its counterpart, a 2-mode network, since in 1-mode networks, vertices can have ties with any other node in the network, while this is not true for 2-mode networks.

It's easy to figure out strong and weak components within our network *via* applying (Net/Components/Weak) commands in Pajek. However, the reason for using option *'weak'* rather than option *'strong'* is that our network is undirected so; we can only use the first option. The results showed that (for n>=2), the network consists only of 883 components. The size of the largest component is 54701 (78.404%), while the size of the next largest component is 13096 (18.770%, not shown here) and the rest of components constitute approximately 10% of the network.

Network diameter, which is the longest shortest path in the network, is 10. This geodesic distance exists only between two users, namely 150578 and 112131. The first guy is 43 years old from Milano, Italy while the other guy is 12 years old from Sydney, Australia. This could be due to the variation in age and the geographic locations of both. The average degree here expresses more cohesive structure and is obtained by dividing the number of edges (*2) by the number of nodes in the network.

We can see that at this time, the network not only has connected components of two or more vertices, but also single-vertex connected components equal to 13096, which means that it includes 'isolates'. This is because the user-user sub-network emerges from a larger network, namely the user-preference network that already contains books having in-degree value equals to 1. When extracting a one-mode subnetwork from a two-mode network, these nodes become 'isolates'. The network has 1875356164 unreachable pairs, which expresses the number of pairs of nodes that do not have a path between them.

4.12. CENTRALITY MEASURES

We want to infer the most potential central people in the network. So, we are going to implement the three measures of centrality: degree centrality, closeness centrality and betweenness centrality. Research has proved that these three measures are highly correlated and give similar results in identifying most important actors in a network (Cheng, 2006, p. 87).

The importance behind identifying most important actors is that it reflects how active the users are. Also, active actors are more likely to establish social ties with a large number of other actors.

To know how these three measures are correlated, let's take a look at a typical example (Fig. **23**). The user in the middle has 4 connected edges, so he has the top degree centrality. Also, he is closer to everyone else than anyone else so, he has the top closeness centrality. And again he lies between each pair of nodes, while others do not, so he has the top betweenness centrality.

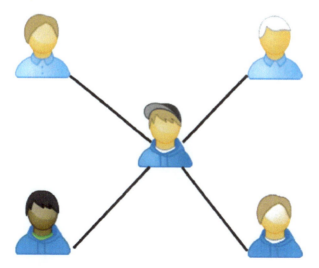

Figure 23: Star-network (centrality measures simplified).

1) Degree Centrality: We are going to find top degree centrality values using the same previously used methods. However, at this time, it doesn't matter whether we apply input, output or all within Pajek since the network is undirected (Fig. **24**).

Figure 24: Circular representation for the degree-centrality measure of the user-user network. The drawing was built based on node (circle) size. The larger the node is, the more central a user in the network (in regard to degree centrality).

Degree centrality statistics of the user-user network are as in Table **16**:

Table 16: Degree centrality statistics of the user-user network

Metric	Value
Dimension	69768
Highest degree centrality value	24026
Lowest degree centrality value	0
Network Input Degree Centralization	0.34307946

We can see that we have nodes with degree centralities equal to 0 because these nodes are 'isolates'.

Degree centrality values of the first ten actors in the user-user network are given in Table **17**:

Table 17: Degree centrality values in the user-user network

Rank	User ID	Degree Centrality	Demographic Info
1.	11676	24026	N/A
2.	16795	8614	Mechanicsville, Maryland, USA, 47 Years Old
3.	95359	8110	Charleston, west Virginia, USA, 33 Years Old
4.	60244	6493	Alvin, Texas, USA, 47 Years Old
5.	204864	6104	Simi valley, California, USA, 47 years Old
6.	104636	5533	Youngstown, Ohio, USA
7.	98391	5480	Morrow, Georgia, USA, 52 years old
8.	35859	5409	Duluth, Minnesota, USA
9.	135149	5283	ft. Pierce, Florida, USA
10.	153662	5281	ft. Stewart, Georgia, USA, 44 years old

The user with the highest degree centrality is ID #11676. However, we can't find any demographic information related to him/her, as it seems that he/she preferred to keep identification information dim. That guy has already occupied position #1 in terms of the people with the highest number of outgoing ties in the mother-network.

That guy has the largest potential social network, as he/she is connected in a direct path to 24026 other actors (neighbors) in the network, which means that he/she shares common opinions about a specific number of book(s) with other 24026 users in the user-user network. This high number of connections reflects the fact that a 1-mode network has a higher density than a 2-mode network since nodes can freely connect to any other node in the same network.

The user in position #2, namely user ID 16795 (47 years old of Maryland, USA), has the second largest potential social network consisting of 8614. However, he/she comes only in rank #9 in a previous statistics about users with the highest number of outgoing ties. This means that even though this guy had fewer number of outgoing ties than the other eight guys, his/her choices were more focused and that he/she could share book preferences with more people, which makes him/her a good candidate to establish a big circle of social relations (of course after our top guy).

2) Closeness Centrality: The concept of closeness centrality depends on the total distance between one vertex and all other vertices, as large distances show lower closeness centrality. Closeness centrality values range from 0 (for isolated vertices) to 1 for the user in-the-middle in the star network since, for a specific vertex, it results from the number of all other vertices in the network divided by the sum of distances between that vertex and all other vertices in the network. Therefore, closeness centrality values are continuous rather than discrete (Cheng, 2006, p. 87). A 3-D representation for the closeness centrality measure of the user-user network can be found in Fig. **25**.

Figure 25: Circular 3-D representation for the closeness centrality measure of the user-user network. All nodes are equally sized.

We can calculate top closeness centrality values by applying (Net/Vector/Closeness/all). Also, we can use any other option rather than "all", namely input or output, since the network is undirected. It takes about 15 hours to calculate closeness centrality values of all vertices in the network. However; it depends mainly on the device specifications. Some overall statistics of closeness centrality measure are given in Table **18**:

Table 18: Overall statistics for the closeness centrality measure of the user-user network

Metric	Value
Dimension	69768
Highest closeness centrality value	0.4926
Lowest closeness centrality value	0.0000
Arithmetic mean	0.2233
Median	0.2661
Standard deviation	0.1220
Network closeness centralization cannot be computed: the network is weakly connected	-

The closeness centrality values of the first ten actors in the user-user network can be found in Table **19**:

Table 19: Highest ten closeness centrality values in the user-user network

Rank	Closeness Centrality	User ID	Demographic Info
1.	0.4926	11676	N/A
2.	0.4021	16795	Mechanicsville, Maryland, USA, 47 years old
3.	0.4011	95359	Charleston, west Virginia, USA, 33 years old
4.	0.3919	60244	Alvin, Texas, USA, 47 years old
5.	0.3906	204864	Simi valley, California, USA, 47 years old
6.	0.3862	35859	Duluth, Minnesota, USA
7.	0.3860	135149	ft. Pierce, Florida, USA
8.	0.3852	104636	Youngstown, Ohio, USA
9.	0.3850	153662	ft. Stewart, Georgia, USA, 44 years old
10.	0.3838	98391	Morrow, Georgia, USA, 52 years old

It is easy to notice that the user (ID= 11676) occupies position #1 in regard to the people with the top closeness centrality values. This is mainly true because he is the top out-degree user, and the top in-degree user.

The rest of actors in the table also appeared in other tables. This reflects their importance at the social level, alongside the ultimate importance of the top-user (namely user ID= 11676).

Network closeness centralization cannot be computed if the network was not strongly connected since there are no paths between all vertices. Therefore, it is impossible to compute the distances between some vertices (De Nooy *et al.*, 2005, p. 128).

3) Betweenness Centrality: While degree and closeness centrality are based on the concept of the reachability of a person, betweenness centrality is based on the idea that a person is more important if he/she was more intermediary in the network. The concept of betweenness centrality is based on geodesics between actors, as a person gets more important if he/she is situated on the geodesics between many pairs of actors in the network. The more a person is a go-between, the more central her/his position in that network is. This reflects the importance of a person being in the middle of social communications of a network and to what extent he/she is needed as a link in the chains of contact in a society.

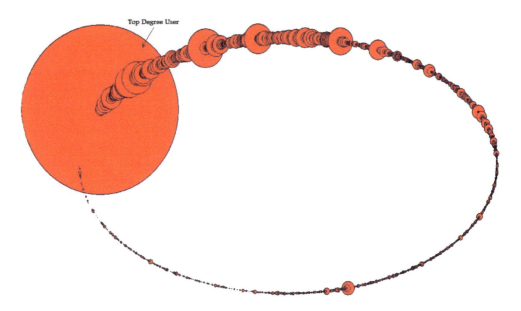

Figure 26: Circular representation for the betweenness-centrality measure of the user-user network. The drawing was built based on node size. The larger the node (circle) is, the more central the user in the network, in regard to betweenness centrality concept

On the other hand, a vertex has betweenness centrality equals to 0 if it is not located between any other vertices in the network, which points out to a weak social role played. Many vertices may not appear in the (Fig. **26**) because they do not mediate between any two vertices, so their betweenness centralities equal zero.

Again, it takes about 15 hours to calculate all betweenness centrality values. However, it depends mainly on the device specifications. Some overall statistics of the betweenness centrality measure can be found in Table **20**:

Table 20: Overall statistics of the betweenness centrality measure in the user-user network

Metric	Value
Dimension	69768
Highest betweenness centrality value	0.1735
Lowest betweenness centrality value	0.0000
Arithmetic mean	0.0000
Median	0.0000
Standard deviation	0.0007
Network betweenness centralization	0.17345915

The betweenness centralities of the first ten actors in the network are given in Table **21**:

Table 21: Betweenness centrality values in the user-user network

Rank	Betweenness Centrality	User ID	Demographic Info
1.	0.1735	11676	N/A
2.	0.0121	98391	Morrow, Georgia, USA, 52 Years Old
3.	0.0094	16795	Mechanicsville, Maryland, USA, 47 Years Old
4.	0.0085	95359	Charleston, west Virginia, USA, 33 Years Old
5.	0.0065	153662	ft. Stewart, Georgia, USA, 44 Years Old
6.	0.0055	204864	Simi valley, California, USA, 47 years old
7.	0.0055	60244	Alvin, Texas, USA, 47 years old
8.	0.0053	23902	London, England, United Kingdom
9.	0.0047	135149	ft. Pierce, Florida, USA
10.	0.0045	104636	Youngstown, Ohio, USA

We can see that all the guys in the table above also appear elsewhere in the study, which reflects their social importance in the community. The top-user is still in rank #1 in the table meaning that he/she lies at the geodesic distances between other pairs, more than any other vertex in the network. This nominates him/her (more than others) to be a candidate person to play many potential brokerage roles in the future.

All the three measures (degree, closeness and betweenness centrality) have showed similar (not necessarily identical) results, which support the notion that all these measures collectively are used to measure most important individuals in a community.

4.13. EGO-NETWORK ANALYSIS

After conducting a comprehensive analysis using some important measures in SNA, we turn our eyes to the top-user (ID= 11676) who occupied the first position in all the previous tests, and try to analyze his/her sub-network (which is called ego-network or ego-centric approach as opposed to the socio-centric approach).

A very useful way to understand complicated networks is to see how they arise from the local connections of individual actors.

We start the analysis by calculating geodesics from the top-user to all other vertices in the user-user network (Table **22**):

Table 22: Geodesic distances from top-degree user to all other users in the user-user network

Cluster	Frequency
0	1
1	24026
2	29088
3	1490
4	86
5	10
Sum	54701
Unknown	15067
Total	**69768**

We can see that the top-degree user can reach 24026 users with only one hop. He/she can reach 29088 other users with two hops, 1490 others with three hops and so on. However, there are other 15067 vertices that can't be reached by ego; in other word they are unreachable in our ego-network, and hence are given the value 999999997 in Pajek's report of distances. In the ego-network, there are unreachable nodes because our user-user network is split up into smaller parts (883 connected components). Cluster (0) means that that ego doesn't need any hop to get to that node, as it is the ego him/her-self.

We can also identify the potential brokerage roles practiced by ego in the user-user network. Brokerage expresses the ability to induce and exploit competition between the other two actors of the triad (a triad consists of a focal person, alter and a third person in addition to the ties among them), and also expresses his/her qualifications to play a subversive role through creating or exploiting conflict between the other two actors in order to control them (De Nooy *et al.*, 2005, p. 145).

Brokerage can be expressed by the 'aggregate constraint' which is the sum of the dyadic constraint on all of a vertex's ties. However, the aggregate constraint has an opposite effect, *i.e.* the more the aggregate constraint, the less the brokerage role an actor can play. We can calculate the brokerage played by ego and other users in the user-user network through applying (Net/Vector/Structural Holes) within Pajek. The implementation gives us the distribution table of aggregate constraints. We give in Table **23**, below, the two extremes:

Table 23: Aggregate constraint of the two extremes in the user-user network

Aggregate Constraint	Value	Representative
Highest Value	1.3203	44726
Lowest Value	0.0007	11676

We see that the top-user (ego) has the lowest aggregate constraint in the user-user network because he/she has the highest out-degree in the mother network, in-degree, betweenness and closeness values in the user-user network. In other words; he/she can perfectly play brokerage.

User brokerage depends mainly on the structural holes within the network which allow a single user to apply his/her strategies. A low constraint on a user indicates many structural holes which may be exploited by him/her. Let's take this little example to illustrate the idea:

Let's take a look at Fig. **27**: in (b), ego can perfectly play the brokerage role between alter and third. Also, he is considered in a powerful position and can profit from the competition between alter and third since the triad is incomplete and that the network has a structural hole. However, ego can't play the same role in (a) because he/she is under a high constraint and the network has no structural holes since it is a complete triad. From that point, we can conclude that the brokerage is related heavily to the presence (or absence) of structural holes (De Nooy *et al.*, 2005, p. 145).

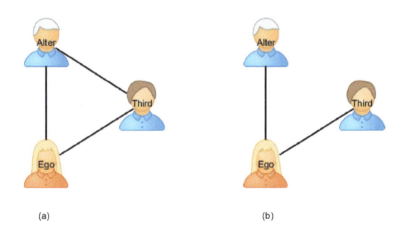

Figure 27: Brokerage roles (a) Ego can barely play the role (b) Ego can perfectly play the role.

The role which the 'constraint' plays in a network has been proven in real life. It has been shown that individuals within an organization with low constraint have more successful jobs. Also, business sectors with low constraint are more profitable.

Extracting sub-graphs, based on a focal actor or set of actors, can be a very useful way to concentrate on a part of a complete network, or the condition of an individual actor.

It's easy to extract the ego-network (which consists of ego, its neighbors and the ties among them) from the user-user network by applying a series of commands within Pajek (Net/K-Neighbours/All). The result is a new network, namely the ego-network (Fig. **28**).

Figure 28: 2-D Representation of the ego-network, extracted from the original user-user network. All labels and edges have been eliminated.

Let's take a look at Table **24** to see a summary for some measures in this network:

Table 24: Overall summary of the ego-network

Metric	Value
Graph Type	Undirected
Number of Neighbors	24026
Number of Edges	2278058
Ego-network Density	0.00789314
Number of Loops	0
Number of Multiple Lines	0
Maximum Geodesic Distance (Diameter)	8
Average Geodesic Distance	2.49241
Average Degree	189.63273121
Ego-network Betweenness Centralization	0.02163385

The network consists of 24026 neighbors (we already passed by this number before). Those neighbors are only the direct ones, *i.e.* who are located at distance one from ego. Also, the number of edges is 2278058. This number represents the relations among vertices around ego.

The density of ego-network expresses the density of ties among its neighbors. The result is 0.00789314 which is higher than the densities of our earlier networks (namely the mother, the user-preference, the user non-preference and the user-user networks), which means that ego-network is quite embedded in dense local substructure. This is because this network is the local network of the user with the top out-degree, top betweenness centrality, top degree centrality, and top closeness centrality.

We must point out here that the above density of ego-network was calculated without ego (*i.e.* the network around ego only). This approach is usually followed by network analysts in order for the analysis to be an indicator of the constraint on ego her/him-self (De Nooy *et al.*, 2005, p. 148).

The ego-network diameter and the average geodesic distance are a little slighter than the user-user network. This is intuitive since the current network is a dense segment within the user-user network.

Also, we notice that ego-network betweenness centralization is 0.02163385 which is lower than what it is in the user-user network. This is because the variation in vertex betweenness centrality in the user-user network is higher than that of the ego-network. A 2-D representation of ego-network betweenness centralization is shown in Fig. **29** below:

Ego-network diameter, that is the maximum geodesic distance between two vertices, is 8. This geodesic distance exists between User ID= 47534 (45 years from Luzern, Switzerland) and User ID= 240418 (34 years old from Barcelona, Spain).

Figure 29: Ego-network betweenness centralization.

4.14. M-SLICE ANALYSIS

A one-mode network induced from a two-mode network prepares the ground to discover many dense structures. One way to detect cohesive subgroups in one-mode networks is to detect m-slice sub-networks. M-slice can be defined as the maximal sub-network in which line multiplicity is equal or greater than m. This technique puts into consideration line multiplicity rather than the number of neighbors (which is defined by the k-core concept). M-slice method comprises allocating network nodes based on their m-slice values, *i.e.* based on the highest ties these nodes are incident (connected) with.

The importance of conducting this type of analysis is that it helps us identify the strongest potential social relations in a network based on the *'participation rate'* between each pair of nodes.

It has been found that the larger the number of interlocks between two users is, the stronger their tie (or relationship) is and the more similar those users are (De Nooy *et al.*, 2005, p. 109).

For example, if woman *i* and women *j* attend 4 events in common, and woman *k* and woman *l* attend the same number of events, we would say that the two pairs are equally close. However, if we knew that woman *k* and woman *l* attended 14 events, we would conclude that woman *k* and woman *l* and more closer to each other than woman *i* and woman *j*. So, we must put into consideration the maximum number of events attended (participation rate) Borgatti and Halgin (2011) put the mathematical proof for this concept.

Different techniques have been proposed to discover similarities among nodes in a network such as correlation (Pearson), similarity function (Cosine) and clustering techniques (PACT, Clique and hypergraph) (Huang, Chung & Chen, 2004).

Back to ego, he/she has 24026 direct neighbors. However, ego is not equally related to all of them. Let's take this little example:

Fig. **30** represents a fragment of the ego-network that connects ego to its 24026 neighbors. Ego's relation with B, for example, is stronger than what it is with A. Also, his/her relation with C is stronger than what it is with B and so on. So, it all depends on tie weights, which determines who is strongly connected to whom.

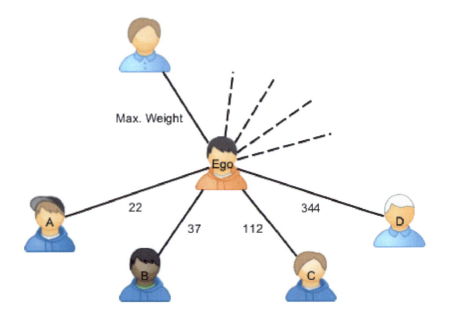

Figure 30: A fragment of the top degree user-network. (Tie values are for demostration purposes only).

We are going to apply the m-slice analysis on the user-user network. But before we conduct the analysis, we will first examine the network in order to find out the distribution of tie weights. The analysis of the user-user network gives us the following results (Table **25**):

Table 25: Distribution of tie weights in the user-user network

I	Tie Weights	Frequency
1	36.0000	24834
2	36.0000 - 8470.3333	3151746
3	8470.3333 - 16904.6667	4
4	16904.6667 - 25339.0000	1
	Total No. of Links	3176585

The results above show that the lowest line multiplicity (line value) is 36 (found in 24834 ties) and the highest line multiplicity is 25339 (found in only 1 tie).

To calculate m-slice values in the user-user network, we will apply a serious of commands within Pajek (Net/Partitions/Valued Core/Threshold and First Step/Input), no matter which option we apply rather than 'input', since this is an undirected network.

From the m-slice frequency tabulation values of the user-user network, we show below the highest five values in addition to the lowest five values (Table **26**):

Table 26: M-slice values in the user-user network

M-Slice	Value	Number of Nodes	Representative
Lowest Five Values	0	13096	-
	36	160	-
	42	525	-
	48	774	-
	49	621	-
Highest Five Values	25339	2	98391, 235105
	16129	1	11676
	9864	1	153662
	9466	1	16795
	7781	1	104636

The results above show that 13096 of the nodes belong to the 0-slice, which means that these nodes are not connected to any node in the network and that those users do not share book preference among them or with any other user. In other words; they are 'isolates'. They represent the weakest potential social components in the user-user network. In fact, they constitute no social components at all (in the context of our measures). It is not likely that those users, in the future, will establish relationships among them by any means or of any type, since they have nothing to share.

We already came by this number when we were examining connected components in the user-user network.

We can also see that the strongest potential social component (which belongs to the 25339-slice) consists of two nodes: 98391 (52 years old from Georgia, USA) and 235105 (46 years old from Missouri, USA). This pair may formulate the most powerful, everlasting, and fast-shaping relationship. Many reasons may stand behind that, for instance: age, occupation, level of education, environment, gender, past experience, marital status and so on.

The top-degree user (user ID= 16129) comes in position #2, although we already saw him/her in a better position in all the previous tests. This could be due to the scattering of his/her preferences.

We can extract stronger and stronger subgroups from any community by removing undesired lines and nodes that do not satisfy our goals. The process will raise the minimum m-slice threshold, which in turn formulate more cohesive groups.

For example, if we remove the 0-slice nodes, the resulting network will consist of 56672 and 3176585 lines. Next, we need to eliminate unnecessary lines. Thus, we obtain more cohesive components.

If we keep going on that process, we will end up with the highest m-slice component, namely 25339-slice that consists of only two nodes (98391, 235105).

Send Orders for Reprints to reprints@benthamscience.net

Social Network Analysis, 2014, 103-111   **103**

CHAPTER 5

Summary and Future Directions

Abstract: In this chapter we will summarize the main concepts that have been addressed throughout this book such as what is SNA, the different types of networks, properties of networks, concepts of graph theory, SNA modeling tools, uses of SNA and other topics with extreme brief. Then we will summarize our main findings that provide answers to questions such as who are the top ten users in the Book Crossing community and what are the top ten popular books and so on.

Keywords: Top ten users, top ten popular books, top ten unpopular books, transitivity, measuring tests, information retrieval, epidemiology, descriptive SNA applications, NodeXL, Gephi, StOCENT, UCINET, network navigation, community structure, clustering, transitivity.

The first part of this book "Fundamentals" has discussed the theoretical concepts of social network analysis. The main objective of SNA is to identify local and global patterns, locate influential entities and examine network dynamics. It focuses on ties among people, organizations and even countries, as these ties combine to form networks. Networks in real life have different shapes and different functionalities. They can be: (i) social networks: A social structure made up of a set of actors and a set of dyadic ties between those actors. Both social networks and social network analysis have their roots in social psychology, sociology, statistics and graph theory, (ii) information networks: the best example here is the World Wide Web, (iii) technological networks: the best two examples here are the Internet and the telephone network, and finally (iv) biological networks that represent patterns of interaction between biological elements.

All these types of networks have the following common properties: (i) the small world effect: means that most pairs of nodes in most networks are connected by short paths, (ii) transitivity (clustering): means that if node A is connected to node B and node B is connected to node C, then there is a high likelihood that node A is also connected to node C, (iii) degree distribution: the probability that a node has a degree equals to k, (iv) network resilience: means that networks are susceptible to node removal. However, they vary in the way they respond to node removal, (v) mixing patterns: means that with which, vertices in a network, pair

Seifedine Kadry and Mohammed Z. Al-Taie

up. For example social networks tend to show assortative mixing patterns behavior while technological and biological networks tend to show disassortative mixing patterns behavior, (vii) community structure: means that groups of vertices have high density of edges existing between groups of nodes, and finally (viii) network navigation: means that in addition to the small-world phenomenon that networks show, people are good at finding paths in networks.

The first article on graph theory, which is heavily related to SNA, appeared in 1736 by Euler, who considered the problem of the Seven Bridges of Koinsberg (now known as Kaliningrad) of how to find a way around Kaliningrad by visiting the seven bridges exactly one time.

A graph is simply a set of points and lines where points are called vertices (or nodes) and lines are called edges (or ties). The number of vertices adjacent to a vertex is called the degree of that vertex. A cut-vertex (or cut point) is a vertex whose removal increases the number of components, and a cut-edge is an edge whose removal also increases the number of components.

Undirected graphs are the ones with edges having no direction while directed graphs (or digraphs) are the ones with edges having direction. A graph in which every two vertices are connected is called connected, otherwise it is called disconnected. A graph is called weighted if each edge is assigned a positive real number called the weight of the edge. A directed graph is *weakly connected* if its underlying graph is connected, while it is *strongly connected* if there is a directed walk from each vertex to each other vertex.

Social network analysis goes back to 1934 when Jacob Moreno put his famous publication "*Who Shall Survive?*" the field was developed due to the efforts made by sociometric analysts, the Harvard researchers and the Manchester anthropologist. Since then, the field has grown dramatically, especially with the revolution of the WWW.

Degree centrality, closeness centrality and betweenness centrality are three measures used within SNA to identify the important individuals in a network. Degree centrality considers the nodes with the highest degrees as the most central ones in the network, while closeness centrality measure considers the vertices with the smallest average length of the roads linking an actor to other actors as the central nodes. Betweenness centrality measure considers the node with the highest number of shortest paths between pairs of nodes that run through that node as the most important individual in a network. Other important measures include cohesive subgroups, components and isolates, structural holes, aggregate constraint, dyadic constraint, geodesic distance and clustering coefficient.

Social network analysis modeling tools are software packages used to identify, represent, analyze or visualize social networks. Examples include: Pajek, a software used for analysis and visualization of large networks, UCINET, StOCENT, Gephi, Network Workbench and NodeXL.

Special-purposes SNA modeling tools are used for specific analysis aims such as identification of subgroups, knowledge networks, hidden populations, kinship networks and structural networks. Examples include: NEGOPY, InFlow and SocioMetric LinkAlyzer, while packages with programming utility include JUNG, iGraph, NetworkX, Prefuse and SNAP.

Since the main use of SNA is to identify patterns, locate influential players and probe network dynamics, there should be either a complete dataset, which is not the case most of the time especially for online social network data, or a sample data where a sample of actors may be taken from the set and inference made about the populations of actors from that sample. We need either a complete data or a sample data to do our analysis. Classical data collection methods include questionnaires, interviews, observations and archival records while data of online nature can be collected in a number of ways: online social networks such as Facebook and Twitter, surveys, and developing custom applications used by participants to share content on ONSs.

Data visualization is a very important tool that helps in the analysis of networks by allowing users to see instantly important structural features.

A graph is the most meaningful way to visualize data especially of large size whereas other visualization methods cannot do successfully. A graph can be in many forms such as: directed, undirected, weighted, orthogonal, grid-based, multigraph, mixed and K-vertex-connected.

In addition to graphs, other visualization tools have been used such as trees, which are undirected graphs where any two vertices are connected by one simple path. A tree could be in any form: polytree, rooted, labeled, recursive, directed, free, binary and ternary.

Matrices are arrays of elements. They consist of rows and columns as the intersection between a column and a row is called a cell. Well-used types of matrices include: column-matrices, row matrices, square matrices, identity matrices, diagonal matrices, symmetric matrices, skew-symmetric matrices, triangle matrices and null matrices. For social network analysis, the main types of matrices used are: adjacency matrices, edge list matrices and adjacency list.

Other visualization tools include maps and hybrid approaches: which are multi-dimensional visualization methods that use both graphs and maps.

The importance of SNA applications have been widely recognized by scientists and researchers. In descriptive SNA applications, the focus is on the structural aspects of the network while in explanative SNA applications, the focus is on explaining how attributes of nodes are dependent on their structural embedding within the network.

SNA has been successfully applied in a number of fields: (i) health: such as investigating the relationship between SNA and the epidemiology and prevention of sexually transmitted diseases, (ii) cybercrime: such as investigating online hacker communities, (iii) business: such as studying the influence of SNA and sentiment analysis in predicting business trends, (iv) animal social networks: through investigating the relationships and the social structures of animal gatherings and the direct and indirect interactions between groups, and (v) communications: such as studying the various structural properties of short message service graphs. Other possible use fields for SNA include: information retrieval, information fusion communities and online terrorist groups.

In the second part of the book "Methodology an Implementation", we have learned how to use techniques of SNA in order to analyze one large online social network, namely bookcrossing.com, which is a place where people around the world meet to give their ratings on books they have read.

To discover the key people in our community, we have applied four measuring tests: The total number of ratings each user has provided, degree centrality test, betweenness centrality test and closeness centrality test. The users who occupied the first ten positions in those four tests are shown in Table **27**:

Table 27: Top ten users within four types of test: Total number of ratings, degree centrality, betweenness centrality and closeness centrality (numbers in cells indicate users IDs)

Rank	Number of Ratings Test	Degree Centrality Test	Betweenness Centrality Test	Closeness Centrality Test
1.	11676	11676	11676	11676
2.	98391	16795	98391	16795
3.	153662	95359	16795	95359
4.	189835	60244	95359	60244
5.	23902	204864	153662	204864
6.	76499	104636	204864	35859
7.	171118	98391	60244	135149
8.	235105	35859	23902	104636
9.	16795	135149	135149	153662
10.	248718	153662	104636	98391

In order to narrow the results above, we will calculate the number of appearance of each user (in each category). For example, the top-user (user ID= 11676) appears in four places so, he/she is in category #4 (A category represents the number of appearances for each user within the list of the ten top users). Also, he/she has occupies the first positions in all these four tests so; he/she gets four points (by multiplying 1*4). That user is in a better position compared to his subsequent fellow (in the table below), namely user ID= 16795, who also belongs to category #4 but obtained 16 points (9+2+3+2=16). As a rule of thumb, we shall suppose the following: the less the number of points is, the higher the rank of that user is.

The overall top ten users within the Book-Crossing community (at the time of the data) are as in Table **28**:

Table 28: Top ten users within the Book-Crossing website based on decomposition

Rank	User ID	Category	Points	Demographic Information
1.	11676	4	4	Null
2.	16795	4	16	Mechanicsville, Maryland, USA, 47 Years Old
3.	98391	4	21	Morrow, Georgia, USA, 52 years old
4.	153662	4	27	ft. Stewart, Georgia, USA, 44 years old
5.	95359	3	10	Charleston, west Virginia, USA, 33 years old
6.	60244	3	15	Alvin, Texas, USA, 47 years old
7.	204864	3	16	Simi valley, California, USA, 47 years old
8.	104636	3	24	Youngstown, Ohio, USA
9.	135149	3	25	ft. Pierce, Florida, USA
10.	23902	2	13	London, England, United Kingdom

The results show that 8 to 9 of actors are from USA and that only 1 to 2 of actors is from a country rather than USA, namely United Kingdom. The results also show that almost half of the actors are in 40s. The lack of more demographic information has stopped us from knowing more about the implications behind users' preferences.

The books that earned the highest number of ratings, whether negative or positive (from 1 to 10 on the rating scale), are shown in Table **29**:

Table 29: The ten books that earned the highest number of ratings (*i.e.* on the scale from 1 to 10)

Rank	Most Rated Books	Author	Year
1.	The Lovely Bones: A Novel	Alice Sebold	2002
2.	Wild Animus	Rich Shapero	2004
3.	The Da Vinci Code	Dan Brown	2003
4.	The Red Tent (Bestselling Backlist)	Anita Diamant	1998
5.	Memoirs of a Geisha: A Novel	Arthur golden	1999
6.	Divine Secrets of the Ya-Ya Sisterhood: A Novel	Rebecca Wells	1997
7.	Harry Potter and the Sorcerer's Stone (Harry Potter (Paperback)	J. K. Rowling	1999
8.	The Secret Life of Bees	Sue Monk Kidd	2002
9.	Where the Heart Is (Oprah's Book Club (Paperback))	Billie Letts	1998
10.	A Painted House	JOHN GRISHAM	2001

Although those books obtain a large number of users' evaluations, they are not necessarily considered as the most preferable books to users. We can say that those books take a wide range of users' interest, and that users have different impressions about these books which in turn pushed them to adopt various perspectives.

The books that earned the highest number of positive ratings (from 6 to 10 on the rating scale) are shown in Table **30**:

Table 30: Top ten popular books

Rank	Most Popular Books	Author	Year
1.	The Lovely Bones: A Novel	Alice Sebold	2002
2.	The Da Vinci Code	Dan Brown	2003
3.	The Red Tent (Bestselling Backlist)	Anita Diamant	1998
4.	Memoirs of a Geisha: A Novel	Arthur golden	1999
5.	Harry Potter and the Sorcerer's Stone (Harry Potter (Paperback))	J. K. Rowling	1999
6.	The Secret Life of Bees	Sue Monk Kidd	2002
7.	Divine Secrets of the Ya-Ya Sisterhood: A Novel	Rebecca Wells	1997
8.	Where the Heart Is (Oprah's Book Club (Paperback))	Billie Letts	1998
9.	Girl with a Pearl Earring	Tracy Chevalier	2003
10.	Angels & Demons	Dan Brown	2000

We can see that eight of the books in the table above also appear within the list of the books that earn the highest number of ratings. Some of these books became the story of cinema movies (*e.g.* the Da Vinci Code). Also, the author "Dan Brown" has two books within this list, namely the book in position #2 and in position #10. This may reflect his significance as a key author in the world of books.

The books that earned the highest number of negative ratings, *i.e.* on a scale from 1-5, are shown in Table **31**:

Table 31: Top ten unpopular books

Rank	Most Unpopular Books	Author	Year
1.	Wild Animus	Rich Shapero	2004
2.	A Painted House	JOHN GRISHAM	2001

3.	The Lovely Bones: A Novel	Alice Sebold	2002
4.	The Pilot's Wife : A Novel	Anita Shreve	1999
5.	The Catcher in the Rye	J. D. Salinger	-
6.	The Red Tent (Bestselling Backlist)	Anita Diamant	1998
7.	The Notebook	Nicholas Sparks	1996
8.	Isle of Dogs	Patricia Cornwell	2001
9.	The Girls' Guide to Hunting and Fishing	Melissa Bank	2000
10.	House of Sand and Fog	Andre, III Dubus	2001

We can see that 2 of the books in the list above also appear in the list of books that earned the highest number of positive ratings (namely books in position #3 and position #6). This gives an indication that users' opinions towards these books scattered across the entire scale and that people were inconsistent about them.

We also looked for the strongest and the weakest social relationships within the hypothetical user-user network by using m-slice type of analysis. The results are shown in Table **32**:

Table 32: Strongest and weakest relationships in the user-user network

Relationship	Weight	Number of Nodes	Representative
Weakest	0	13096	-
Strongest	25339	2	98391, 235105

We can see that the weakest relationships have weights equal to 0, which means that those entities represent isolated nodes. The number of the weakest relationships is 13069. Also, the strongest potential relationship has a weight equals to 25339 represented only by one entity existing between two nodes (98391 & 235105).

We have seen that techniques of social network analysis can be applied in the social domain to discover many structural sides of the community. We found that centrality measures (degree, closeness and betweenness) are among the most powerful techniques that are used to explore key players in a specific community. The degree prestige measure can be used to discover most prestigious elements in a community. Affiliation network analysis can be used to extract possible social relationships within a two-mode network. We have also seen that specific users can dominate the traffic of roads in a specific community, and that he/she can perform many brokerage roles between any two actors. At the social level, some people are more qualified to establish a spider net of communications due to his/her privileged position in the network, while others prefer to keep playing the audience.

We can further extended our analysis to include other online social networks, such as eBay, Facebook or MySpace. Any website where people are able to rate items is a good place to extract the potential social relations from. Many websites, these days, give a space to visitors to rate the items they have examined in that community.

We can build a map of user preferences that will help us further predict user behaviors and even give recommendations to other customers.

We can further make the operation more autonomous and develop an agent that can automatically visit a specific website and recursively extract huge amount of data (maybe bigger than the current one). But, at the same time, we should keep in mind to preserve privacy.

REFERENCES

Abraham, J., Hassanien, A. E. & Snasel, V. (Eds.). (2010). *Computational social network analysis: Trends, tools and research advances*. London: Springer.

Al-Taie, M. and Kadry, S. (2012). Applying Social Network Analysis to Analyze a Web-Based Community. *In the International Journal of Advanced Computer Science and Applications (IJACSA)*, 3(2), 29-41.

Bakk, M. A. Z. (2010). *Social network analysis in DBpedia*. (Master's thesis, University of Wien).

Barale, C. (2010). A social network approach to sheep movement and leadership. *Applications of Social Network Analysis ASNA, Zurich*.

Batagelj, V. & Mrvar, A. (2003). Pajek: Analysis and visualization of large networks. *Graph Drawing Software*, 77-103.

Berger-Wolf, T., Fischhoff, I., Rubenstein, D. I., Sundaresan, S. R. & Tantipathananandh, C. (2010). Dynamic Analysis of Social Networks of Equids. *Applications of Social Network Analysis ASNA, Zurich*.

Bohn, J., Feinerer, I., Hornik, K. & Mair, P. (2011). Content-Based social network analysis on mailing lists. *The R Journal*, 3(1), 11-18.

Borgatti, S. P. & Foster, P. C. (2003). The network paradigm in organizational research: A review and typology. *Journal of Management*, 29(6), 991-1013.

Borgatti, S.P. and Halgin, D. (2011). Analyzing Affiliation Networks. In Carrington, P. and Scott, J. (Eds.), *Handbook of Social Network Analysis*. SAGE Publications.

Carrington, P. J., Scott, J. & Wasserman, S. (Eds.). (2005). *Models and methods in social network analysis*. New York, NY: Cambridge University Press.

Caschera, M. C., Ferri, F., & Grifoni, P. (2008). SIM: A dynamic multidimensional visualization method for social networks. *PsychNology Journal, 6*(3), 291-320.

Cheng, B. (2006). *Using social network analysis to investigate potential bias in editorial peer review in core journals of comparative/international education* (Doctoral dissertation).

Cortes, C., Mohri, M. & Rastogi, A. (2007). An alternative ranking problem for search engines. *Proceedings of the 6th International Conference on Experimental Algorithms*, 4525, 1-22.

Coscia, M., Giannotti, F. & Pensa, R. (2009). Social network analysis as knowledge discovery process: A case study on digital bibliography. *International Conference on Advances in Social Network Analysis and Mining, ASONAM*, 279 – 283.

De Nooy, W. (2003). Social network analysis, graph theoretical approaches to. *In: R. A. Meyers (Ed.), Springer Encyclopedia of Complexity and System Science,* 8231-8245.

De Nooy, W., Mrvar, A. & Batagelj, V. (2005). *Exploratory social network analysis with Pajek*. New York, NY: Cambridge University Press.

Doshi, L., Krauss, J., Nann, S. & Gloor P. (2009). Predicting movie prices through dynamic social network analysis. *Elsevier Science Journal*, 2(4), 6423-6433.

Duijn, M. A. J. V. & Vermunt, J. K. (2006). What is special about social network analysis? *Methodology European Journal of Research Methods for the Behavioral and Social Sciences*, 2, 2-6.

Ereteo, G. (2011). *Semantic social network analysis* (Doctoral dissertation).

Ereteo, G., Buffa, M., Gandon, F., Grohan, P., Leitzelman, M., and Sander, P. (2008). A state of the art on the social network analysis and its applications on a semantic web. *Social Data on the Web (SDoW2008)*.

Freeman, L. C. (2004). *The development of social network analysis: A study in the sociology of science.* South Carolina: BookSurge, LLC.

Friemel, T. N. (Eds.). (2008). *Why Context Matters: Applications of Social Network Analysis.* Germany.

Fruchterman, T. M. J. & Reingold, E. M. (1991), Graph drawing by force-directed placement. *Software: Practice and Experience*, 21, 1129–1164.

Gardy, J. L., Johnston, J. C., Sui, S. J. H., Cook, V. J., Shah, L., Brodkin, E., Rempel, S., Moor, R., Zhao, Y., Holt, R., Varhol, R., Birol, I., Lem, M., Sharma, M. K., Elwood, K., Jones, S. J. M., Brinkman, F. S. L., Brunham, R. C. & Tang, P. (2011). Whole-Genome sequencing and social network analysis of Tuberculosis outbreak. *The New England Journal of Medicine, 364*(8), 730-739.

Gephi, open source graph visualization software. Features. Retrieved, December 3, 2011, from http://gephi.org/features/

Goldenberg, A. (2007). *Scalable graphical models for social networks* (Doctoral dissertation).

Hanneman, R. A. & Riddle, M. (2005). *Introduction to social network methods.* Retrieved from http://faculty.ucr.edu/~hanneman/nettext/Introduction_to_Social_Network_Methods.pdf

Hatala, J. P. (2006). Social network analysis in human resources development: A new methodology. *Human Resources Development Review, 5*(1), 45-71.

Hawe, P., Webster, C. & Shiell, A. (2004). A glossary of terms for navigating the field of social network analysis. *J Epidemiol Community Health,* 58, 971-975.

Holzer, R., Malin, B. & Sweeney, L. (2005). Email alias detection using social network analysis. *Proceedings of the ACM SIGKDD Workshop on Link Discovery (LinkKDD).*

Huang, B. & Jebara, T. (2010). Exact graph structure estimation with degree priors. *International Conference on Machine Learning and Applications,* 111–118.

Huang, Z., Chung, W. & Chen, H. (2003). A graph model for e-commerce recommender systems. *Journal of the American Society for Information Science and Technology, 55*(3), 259-274.

Kakimoto, T., Kamei, Y., Ohira, M. & Matsumoto K. (2006). Social network analysis on communication for knowledge collaboration in OSS communities. *Proceedings of the 2nd International Workshop on Supporting Knowledge Collaboration in Software Development KCSD2006,* 1-7.

Kim, K-J. & Ahn, H. (2012). Hybrid Recommender Systems Using Social Network Analysis. *World Academy of Science, Engineering and Technology.*

Kramer, T., Hildenbrand, T. & Acker, T. (2009). Enabling social network analysis in distributed collaborative software development. *Software Engineering (Workshops)*, 255-266.

Lappas, T., Liu, K. & Terzi, E. (2009). Finding a Team of Experts in Social Network. *KDD '09 Proceedings of the 15th ACM SIGKDD international conference on Knowledge discovery and data mining, 467-476.*

Lowd, D. & Davis, J. (2010). Learning Markov network structure with decision trees. *Proceedings of the 10th IEEE International Conference on Data Mining (ICDM).*

Lu, Y., Polgar, M., Luo, X. & Cao, Y. (2010). Social network analysis of a criminal hacker community. *Journal of Computer Information Systems, 51*(2), 31.

Lucas, J. P., Segrera, S. & Moreno, M. N. (2008). Comparing the use of traditional and associative classifiers towards personalized recommendations. *In Proceedings of SEKE'2008*, 607-612.

Marin, A. & Wellman, B. (2010). Social network analysis: An introduction. Forthcoming in Carrington, P. and Scott, J. (Eds.), *Handbook of Social Network Analysis.* SAGE Publications.

Meneely, A., Williams, L., Snipes, W. & Osborne J. (2008). Predicting failures with developer networks and social network analysis. *Proceedings of the 16th ACM SIGSOFT International Symposium on Foundations of software engineering ACM.*

Mika, P. (2007). *Social networks and the semantic web.* New York, NY: Springer.

Nardi, B. A., Whittaker, S., Isaacs, E., Creech, M., Johnson, J., Hainsworth, J. (2001). ContactMap: Integrating Communication and Information Through Visualizing Personal Social Networks. *Forthcoming in the communications of the ACM.*

Network Workbench. About. Retrieved, December 3, 2011, from http://nwb.cns.iu.edu/about.html

NetworkX. Overview-NetworkX 1.6 documentation. Retrieved, December 3, 2011, from Lusseau, D. & Newman, M. E. J. (2004) http://networkx.1an1.gov/

Newman, M. E. J. & Lusseau, D. (2004). Identifying the role that individual animals play in their social network. *Proc. R. Soc. London B (Suppl.) 271, S477-S481.*

Newman, M. E. J. (2010), *Networks: An Introduction.* New York: Oxford University Press.

NodeXL: Network overview, discovery and exploration for Excel. NodeXL features. Retrieved, December 3, 2011, from http://nodexl.codeplex.com/

Otte, E. & Rousseau, R. (2002). Social network analysis: A powerful strategy, also for the information sciences. *Journal of Information Science, 28*(6), 441-453.

Pajek: Program for analysis and visualization of large networks. (2011, September 24). Reference manual.

Papadimitriou, A., Katsaros, D. & Manolopoulos, Y. (2010). Social Network Analysis and its Applications in Wireless Sensor and Vehicular Networks. *Lecture Notes of the Institute for Computer Sciences, Social Informatics and Telecommunications Engineering Volume 26, 2010, pp. 411-420.*

Penuel, W. R., Sussex, W., Korbak, C. & Hoadley, C. (2006). Investigating the potential of using social network analysis in educational evaluation. *American Journal of Evaluation, 27*(4), 437-451.

Perisse, A. R. S. & Nery, J. A. da C. (2007). The relevance of social network analysis on the epidemiology and prevention of sexually transmitted diseases. *Cad. Saude Publica,* 3, 5361-5369.

Reffay, C. & Chanier, T. (2003). How social network analysis can help to measure cohesion in collaborative distance-learning. *Designing for change in networked learning environments In international conference on computer support for collaborative learning,* 343-352.

Regan, E. (2009) Networks: Structure and Dynamics. *In: Meyers RA, editor in chief. Encyclopedia of Complexity and System Science. Springer; 2009 (SBN-13: 978-0-387-75888-6).*

Ricci, F., Rokach, L., Shapira, B. and Kantor, P. B. (Eds.). (2011). *Recommender Systems Handbook.* New York, NY: Springer.

Scott, J. (2000). *Social Network Analysis: A handbook* (2nd). London: SAGE publications, Ltd.

Serrat, O. (2009). *Social Network Analysis.* Asian Development Bank ADB.

Shani, G., Chickering, M. & Meek, C. (2008). Mining recommendations from the web. In Proceedings of the 2008 ACM conference on Recommender systems (RecSys '08). ACM, New York, NY, USA, 35-42.

SNAP Stanford Network Analysis Project. Retrieved, December 3, 2011, from http://snap.stanford.edu/

Social network analysis: Theory and applications. Retrieved from http://train.ed.psu.edu/WFED-543/SocNet_TheoryApp.pdf

Stockman, F. N. (2004). What binds us when with whom? Content and structures in social network analysis. *Extended version of keynote at the SUNBELT XXIV. International social network conference, Portoroz (Slovenia).*

Sun, H., Peng, Y., Chen, J., Liu, C. & Sun, Y. (2011). A new similarity measure based on adjusted Euclidean distance for memory-based collaborative filtering. *Journal of Software, 6*(6).

Tang, L. & Liu, H. (2010). Graph mining applications to social network analysis. *The Kluwer International Series on Advances in Database Systems,* 40, 487-513.

Tomar, V., Asani, H., Karandikar, A., Chander, V., Agrawal, S. & Kapadia, P. (2010). Social Network Analysis of the Short Message Service. *Communications (NCC), 2010 National Conference on.* DOI: 10.1109/NCC.2010.5430162.

Tsvetovat, M. & Kouznetsov, A. (2011). *Social network analysis for startups.* California, CA: O'Reilly Media, Inc.

Valente, T. W. (2010). *Social networks and health: Models, methods and applications.* New York, NY: Oxford University Press.

Wasserman, S., & Faust, K. (1994). *Social network analysis: Methods and applications.* Cambridge: Cambridge University Press.

Weng, L., Zhang, Y., Zhou, Y., Yang, L. T., Tian, P. & Zhong, M. (2009). A joint web resource recommendation method based on category tree and associate graph. *Journal of Universal Computer Science, 15*(12), 2387-2408.

Wey, T., Blumstein, D., Shen, W. & Jordan, F. (2008). Social network analysis of animal behavior: a promising tool for the study of sociality. *Animal Behaviour Volume 75, Issue 2, February 2008, Pages 333–344.*

Xu, Y., Ma, J., Sun, Yonghong, Hao, J., Sun, Yongqiang, & Zhao, Y. (2009). Using social network analysis as a strategy for e-commerce recommendation. *PACIS Proceedings, 106.*

Yang, C. C., & Ng, T. D. (2007). Terrorism and crime related weblog social network: Link, content analysis and information visualization. *Intelligence and Security Informatics, IEEE,* 55-58.

Zhang, X., Fuehres, H. & Gloor P. A. (2010). Predicting stock market indicators through twitter "I hope it was not as bad as I fear". *Anxiety Journal,* 1-8.

Zhang, Y., Cao, B. & Yeng, D. Y. (2010). Multi-Domain collaborative filtering. *Proceedings of the Twenty-Sixth Conference Annual Conference on Uncertainty in Artificial Intelligence,* 725–732.

Ziegler, C. N., McNee, S. M., Konstan J. A. & Lausen, G. (2005). Improving recommendation lists through topic diversification. *WWW '05 Proceedings of the 14th international conference on World Wide Web.*

Index

A

Affiliation networks 68, 82, 112

Animal social networks 56,63-64,106

B

Binary operations 36, 44

Biological networks 3, 6-7, 104

Blogs 3-4

Bookcrossing 68, 107

Brokerage roles 22, 68, 94-96, 111

C

Centrality measures 59, 64, 68, 87, 110

Clustering 7, 21, 23, 33, 100, 103, 105

Collaborative learning 56, 63, 114

Community structure 7, 34, 103-104

Cybercrime 56, 61, 106

D

Data pre-processing 68, 71

Data sampling 36

Degree distribution 3, 7, 56, 65, 103

Deployed applications 36, 38

Descriptive SNA 103, 106

Dijkstra's algorithm 36, 46

Distance-learning 56, 63, 114

E

Ego-centered sampling 36, 55

Epidemiology 56, 60, 61, 103, 106, 114

F

FAOF 56-57

www.ingramcontent.com/pod-product-compliance
Lightning Source LLC
Chambersburg PA
CBHW041429050326
40690CB00002B/476